Our Debt to Greece and Rome

EDITORS
GEORGE DEPUE HADZSITS, PH.D.

DAVID MOORE ROBINSON, PH.D., LL.D.

GREEK RELIGION AND ITS SURVIVALS

BY
WALTER WOODBURN HYDE

COOPER SQUARE PUBLISHERS, INC.
NEW YORK
1963

Published 1963 by Cooper Square Publishers, Inc.
59 Fourth Avenue, New York 3, N. Y.
Library of Congress Catalog Card No. 63-10268

PRINTED IN THE UNITED STATES OF AMERICA

EDITORS' PREFACE

THE SUBJECT of ancient Greek religion is so very large, in all of its manifestations, that the influence of Greek religion can hardly be treated adequately in a single volume in this Series.

Therefore, besides Professor Hyde's book, those on Mythology, Folklore and the Philosophies of the Greeks will further indicate the influence of ancient Greek religion on religious life and thought of later days.

The nature of Christianity in Greek lands is one of the most interesting phenomena and reveals very clearly the depth and the power of *ancient* Greek religious thinking and feeling which completely permeate the *modern* expressions. Our debt to Greece is amazingly disclosed in this field of aspiration, but it remains to be seen whether Greek Christianity will eventually extricate itself from that legacy of superstition that has been so harmful and avail itself only of the nobler qualities of Greek religion. This book may draw the line

[vii]

between the good and the bad more sharply than has been done before and thus point the way.

The Series, "Our Debt to Greece and Rome," is concerned with a dual purpose, not only of defining the nature of our inheritance but also of weaving into the life of to-day, more consciously, those elements that are of permanent worth for the life of the twentieth century.

CONTENTS

CHAPTER   PAGE

       EDITORS' PREFACE   vii

     I. SOME ASPECTS OF ANCIENT GREEK
           RELIGION   3

    II. THE INFLUENCE OF GREEK RELI-
           GION ON EARLY CHRISTIANITY:
           THE GREEK GODS TURNED SAINTS   41

   III. THE GREEK CHURCH FESTIVALS . .   86

   IV. DIVINATION AND SACRIFICE   116

    V. DÆMONOLOGY: NEREIDS, GENII,
           GIANTS, AND CALLICANTZARI . . .   135

   VI. DÆMONOLOGY: LAMIAS, VAMPIRES,
           AND WERE-WOLVES   175

  VII. DESTINY, GUARDIAN ANGELS, DEATH,
           AND THE LIFE HEREAFTER . . .   193

       NOTES   225

       BIBLIOGRAPHY   228

GREEK RELIGION
AND ITS SURVIVALS

GREEK RELIGION AND ITS SURVIVALS

I. SOME ASPECTS OF ANCIENT GREEK RELIGION

THE RELIGION of the ancient Greeks had a long and varied history. It continued on the higher plane of anthropomorphic polytheism for many centuries, back of which extended many more of a cruder animistic past. During its whole development it was quite unchecked by tradition or revelation or by dogma. It adapted itself pliantly to the political, social, and intellectual changes in the evolution of the most gifted of peoples, continually borrowing and assimilating new and foreign ideas. From the sixth century B. C. onwards it was profoundly influenced by poets, philosophers, and artists. In brief, Greek religion was part and parcel of Greek civilization, showing the same mobility, love of freedom, and spirit of progress which we as-

sociate with all other phases of that culture.
And long after the political greatness of
Greece had vanished, Greek religion was destined to influence Christianity by which it was
to be superseded. Nor is its influence yet dead.
For, as we shall see in the following chapters,
many survivals of Hellenic beliefs and practices can still be traced among the Greeks of
to-day as a sort of cryptic paganism under the
guise of Christianity.

In this introductory chapter we shall briefly
discuss some of the characteristic aspects of
this religion in its developed form in the fifth
and fourth centuries B. C. We shall find that
it differed essentially from most of the religions
which dominated the ancient world or those
which demand the reverence of mankind in our
day. We are particularly struck by the absence of certain ideas which are common and
fundamental to most religions. While these
generally emphasize certain dogmas, the religion of the Greeks was primarily not a matter of belief at all, but only of practice. It had
no dogmas, no creeds, no *summa theologiæ*.
It had no sacred books to prove an obstacle to intellectual progress. The absence
of such books was not only the expression,

[4]

but the condition of Greek religious freedom. Greek religion never consecrated, as divinely appointed, certain ideas which belonged to a stage of its development only. The Greeks had, to be sure, certain hymns to the gods, such as the *Homeric Hymns*. They had certain prayer formulæ for special occasions, such as the Athenian rain-prayer. They had elaborate rituals at various shrines for different festivals, time-honored and punctiliously carried out. Even certain views about the gods, crystallized into legends, enjoyed exceptional sanctity. But even if in this sense Homer and Hesiod to some extent represented orthodoxy, their poems never formed a Bible and were never regarded as the word of the gods. The Homeric poems, while they give us an unforgettable picture of the human gods, whose forms are statuesque in their definiteness, were secular and not religious. Their authority was, to be sure, enormous in fixing for centuries the general outline of ideas about the gods and the hereafter, but these poems were never binding on men's beliefs. The Greeks never felt any limitation to their religious imagination and curiosity.

The Greeks never had a religious founder,

nor felt the need of a reformer. Great teachers arose, such as the traditional Orpheus, to advocate doctrines and rules of conduct, but none was strong enough to dominate the popular imagination by the authority of an *ipse dixit*. Moreover, the Greeks never had any idea of a general revelation of the divine will, no story of the origin of the world imposed by authority. Just because of the absence of such a revelation Greek religion never developed into a canonical system to hamper scientific curiosity. In Greece there was always a tendency to subordinate religion to civil authority. The City-State was supreme in controlling religion. It appointed the priests as state officials; it established and supervised the temples and altars, and it administered religious law in the State courts. Thus, the priests, chosen by lot or by the assembly, were never the final authorities in religion. They never formed powerful castes, as in Egypt and India, able to silence religious curiosity. No Greek state ever became theocratic. If the religious unit became larger than that of the City-State, a more extended organization, known as an *amphictyony,* carried on the inter-state religion. The priests were never looked

upon as holy, nor had they any special train-
ing. Physical perfection seems to have been
the chief requirement of their office. They
were not clergymen, for they had no parish and
gave no moral instruction. They merely performed the shrine service, a ritual which was
the result of centuries of growth, and which
was always changing and tending toward, but
never requiring, unity of belief. It never re-
tarded secular advance or moral progress. On
the contrary, speculation and progress were regarded as divine attributes. The Greeks never
felt the need of intermediaries between themselves and their man-made gods.

The political particularism of the Greek
City-State, the result of tradition and especially of the configuration of the Balkan peninsula, where isolated valleys are marked off by
a network of intersecting hills, was reflected in
Greek religion. As each state had its own con-
stitution and laws, so it had its own worship
and its own gods. As there was no national
state down to Macedonian days, there was no
national religion; rather there existed a great
diversity of cults—the chief authority in religious matters being the local shrine tradition.
A few shrines, such as Delphi and Delos, slowly

became recognized by the whole Greek world and exercised a certain control over conduct. But such centers were exceptional and seldom made for unity of religious ideas or conformity in ritual. In short, everything in Greece, physical environment, differences in blood, tradition, dialect, customs, tended to variety in states as in individuals, and this variety was nowhere more prominent than in religion. So Greek religion was a very complex thing, which, owing to the absence of any theological system, never became completely harmonized. Beliefs remained vague and varied. But amid all these local and individual variations we may still trace a certain resemblance in the religious psychology of the Greek states, an unconscious tending toward similar beliefs and practices. As a whole, then, Greek religion had a physiognomy of its own, just as did Greek literature and art. Its salient features were common to the whole spiritual expression of the race.

The absence of a founder, revelation, a binding theology, sacerdotalism, and uniformity resulted in great freedom. Every Greek felt free to believe what he would. From a remark of the Platonic Socrates we infer that the Athenians cared little what a man believed, if he were only punctilious in the public worship and did not proselyte. Freedom of thought, however, did not mean that one could teach atheism, introduce new gods, damage sacred property, or deride the public worship. Aristophanes ridiculed the gods on the stage and Euripides made them detestable, but no one could openly proclaim disbelief in them or refuse to join in the public worship without becoming subject to the law of the state. Socrates was said to be punctilious in adhering to all the details of worship. But no Greek was afraid of being cast out of the synagogue or priesthood for heterodox views, if only he refrained from publicly teaching doctrines at variance with those accepted by his state. Before the days of Alexander it was difficult and dangerous to introduce foreign cults into Greece. But, despite its conservatism, so largely imposed by the state, the story of Greek religion contains only a short chapter of religious intolerance. Anaxagoras, the philosopher, Protagoras, the sophist, Euripides, the poet, and Aristotle were either prosecuted for impiety or voluntarily left Athens. Socrates was the only Greek martyr. When he had

reached the age of seventy years, known everywhere for his uprightness of character, he was
haled into court as an atheist and corrupter of
youth, and was put to death. In most of the
cases cited, the motives of prosecution were
personal and political rather than religious.
The slaying of Socrates was unique and a stain
upon freedom-loving Athens, for he was the
greatest glory of the city which saw fit to kill
him. But even here religious intolerance had
little to do with the crime; it was rather his
supposed oligarchical views and the immediate
circumstances of his trial which were responsible for the strange verdict.

One feature sadly missing in this religion was
the sense of duty which a man should feel toward his fellow-men. Greek religion was concerned almost entirely with men's duty to the
gods, and no other religious system shows so
complete a separation of religion and morality
—ideas which tended to unite only in late antiquity, and which in Christianity are indis-
soluble. The Greek gods were regarded as
neither perfect nor holy; in character and
power they were removed only a little way from
men. The example set by them was rarely, if
ever, appealed to by Greek moralists before the

time of Plato. They were fabled to have fought in battle with men, to have guided men on their journeys, and to have broken bread with them. They were believed to have married or had amours with mortals. After the heroic period, when heroes were thought to have conversed directly with the gods, the latter still spoke to men through oracles. Men dedicated temples to them, offered them food sublimated by the vapor rising from sacrificial animals, and carved them in stone, bronze, and gold and ivory. Men regarded the gods as swayed by like passions and ambitions as themselves. The gods could deceive men, hold their anger against them, be cruel and vindictive toward them, as they also could be friendly and helpful. In short, in their dealings with men, the gods followed the ordinary Greek rule of ethics, "Love your friends and hate your enemies." The idea of deifying great men, which assumed such proportions in the Hellenistic Age, is merely an evidence of the human character of the gods.

The immorality imputed to the gods in legend was a serious obstacle to the ethical progress of the Greeks. This was a fact recognized by poets and thinkers. Greek morality was derived, therefore, not from Greek religion, but from social conditions. But to the loftier minds, the religious teachers of Greece, the gods became the guardians of unwritten law and the guides of conduct. Sophocles could say that "the gods never lead us into evil." Euripides could go farther and say that "if the gods do anything evil, they are not gods." [1] Certain sects, such as the Orphics, did inculcate morality and preached purification from sin, even if the means to such ends were generally ritualistic cleansing and the avoidance of certain foods. Participation in many of the mysteries promised blessings in the life hereafter, but such promises were not dependent upon having lived a blameless life. Rohde rates spiritual ecstasy as the highest manifestation of religious feeling. This was the purpose of the Dionysiac orgies, but it was certainly not conducive to Greek morality, since it was often attained by physical means, such as licentious dancing, the inhalation of vapors, and even drunkenness. We have only to recall the *Bacchanals* of Euripides, which is a glorious literary monument to the sort of spiritual elevation thus produced. Plato derided Musæus for forming no loftier conception of heaven than "eternal drunkenness." How difficult it was for Christianity to bring the Greeks of a later period to the Christian level of morality is shown by St. Paul's rebuke of the Corinthians for having made the communion service an occasion for gluttony and drunkenness.

Throughout the historical period Greek religion was frankly polytheistic. The tendency toward monotheism was found only in the philosophical schools. In fact, the number of gods received into the pantheon steadily grew from the end of the fifth century B. C. onwards. Thus we find greater complexity at the end of paganism than in any preceding century. Nor did the new gods supersede the old; at best they were merely superimposed upon them, so that religious inconsistency was ever rife. The summary of Euripides' doubts is found in the reflection of Orestes that "in things divine great confusion reigns." [2] Side by side with higher ideas there often lingered more primitive ones, the survivals of an animistic past with its vague personification of natural forces and its simpler ritual. In later days also an older god was often clothed with a different character, nor was this change always for the better. Pausanias, who travelled over Greece in the age of the Antonines, records many traces of such primitive cults that still survived in his day, such as the worship of unwrought stones as divinities, and the survival of human sacrifice in the cult of Zeus on Mount Lycæus in Arcadia. Aphrodite was worshipped as the "Heavenly" and as the "Popular"—in the one cult friendly to marriage and chastity, in the other hostile. In one form of his worship Dionysus, the wine-god, was allied to the austere systems of Orphism and the Eleusinian mysteries, but such connections never purged the primitive cult of its orgies and savage rites, especially the *omophagia,* in which his drunken revellers rent a living bull to pieces with their teeth and ate its flesh raw, in commemoration of the mythical death of the god at the hands of his enemies. But we can trace a monotheistic tendency among the deeper minds of Greece from Xenophanes onwards. In fact, Höffding is right in saying that the idea of an organized hierarchy of gods under the rule of one is a "station on the way from polytheism to monotheism." We can trace the evolution of Zeus from the Homeric conception of him as king of gods and men and master of the thunder and lightning, powers which he inherited from his prototype, the old Indo-European sky-god, to the time when finally his majesty called forth the grand tribute of Cleanthes as the "greatest of gods, god with many names, god ever-ruling, and ruling all things"; but the journey from Homer to such an impassioned outburst of religious feeling is one of many centuries.

The Greek polytheistic view of deity, then, was in utter contrast with that of the Jews as expressed, for example, in the 139th *Psalm*: "If I ascend up into heaven, thou art there: if I make my bed in Sheol, behold, thou art there." For, instead of an all-embracing God, here is a pantheon of many gods, each endowed with peculiar powers and attributes. All nature teemed with personal gods and inferior dæmons or potencies. Subject only to Destiny, that vague and impersonal belief as found in the *Iliad*, but later in the *Odyssey* pluralized and personified as the "stern spinning women who drew off the spindles for Odysseus at his birth," these gods have full control of nature, dwelling in the air above, in the sea, on and beneath the earth. Although they are immortal, they are not the creators of the world, for they have a beginning, as is related in various cosmogonies and dynastic legends. They are innumerable in rank from Zeus down. In later days the distinction between gods and dæmons was more and more emphasized, the latter being regarded as less powerful and more often unfriendly to men. Like other primitive races the early Greeks with their vivid imaginations peopled every remarkable spot with living beings, every stream, valley, mountain, cave, and forest. The supernatural beings who inhabited such spots, the nymphs of water and land, the satyrs and fauns, the river-gods and dryads, were merely the expressions of the animistic view of nature which the classical Greeks had inherited from their remote ancestors and beyond which they could never go. Their rationalizing genius, however, kept them from falling into the gross and repulsive absurdities which are so common in Oriental superstition. It is no wonder that these beings should gradually have taken on such beautiful forms in the imagination of so artistic a race.

As we first meet these gods in Homer, they have finally, after long ages of development, received their definite forms and attributes which were continued to the end of antiquity. Even after a more spiritual conception had been evolved of the god-head, belief in this naïve anthropomorphism was maintained. Thus Plato, in the *Phœdrus,* says: "But we, though we have never seen or rightly conceived a god, imagine an immortal being which has both a soul and a body, which are united for all time." [3]   Homer, therefore, represents the end and not the beginning of a long evolution. Nor can we say when, in this development, the Greeks reached the anthropomorphic stage. We know that the Indo-Europeans before their dispersion believed in gods who were not personal beings, and that consequently the Hellenes must have reached polytheism in Greece, and that the Olympians were developed out of natural phenomena and the heavenly bodies. The later Greeks were quite conscious of the fact that their primitive religion had been the simple worship of the more remarkable nature objects and striking phenomena. Thus Plato, in the *Cratylus,* suspected that the sun, moon, stars, heaven, and earth were the only gods known to the "aboriginal Hellenes."

In Homer the gods are almost completely anthropomorphic. They are sharply defined personalities, colossal men and women, fairer and stronger than mortals, but conceived in

[17]

their glorified image. This anthropomorphism is at times very naïve, there being hardly a limit to the degree in which the poet reproduces human nature in his gods. They were so humanly conceived that later artists could embody in their work ideas straight from Homer's descriptions. This is shown by the tradition handed down by Strabo that the well-known lines from the first book of the *Iliad*, which close the scene in which Thetis importunes Zeus to honor her son Achilles, suggested to Phidias the concept of his most famous work, the colossal chryselephantine statue of the god at Olympia. These gods can work wonders and take on any shape they will, although their power of transformation never degenerates into the grotesque, but follows the usual Greek rule of "moderation." They are like men in the necessities of their being, requiring ambrosia and nectar to sustain them, sleep and "a place in the sun." Their chief occupation, apart from meddling with the affairs of men, is feasting. They feel both pleasure and pain, and are swayed by the same passions of love and hate, jealousy and revenge, as men. In short, Olympus merely reflects earthly notions of ethics, as it also does of politics. The Ionian

[18]

bards did not always take the gods seriously
or reverently, but often in their lays used them
for ornament and even burlesque. Especially
is this true of Zeus and Hera. While Zeus is
as grand as his thunder in his natural aspect, he
falls far below mortals when viewed as father
and husband, and Hera is pictured as anything
but a dutiful consort. In a passage at the end
of the first book of the *Iliad,* Zeus threatens his
spouse with laying his "untouchable hands
upon her," and in another, Hera boxes the ears
of Artemis. Quarrels are frequent on Olympus
and the gods often mingle in human frays.
They wear the armor of men, drive horses and
chariots to battle, and are wounded. In the
Iliad Ares is a cowardly Thracian, while Aphrodite is rebuked for entering the struggle
before Troy. Athena attacks the god of war
during the mêlée with a stone, until Aphrodite
leads him away by the hand "groaning continually." Even then Athena pursues and
wounds him. Ares and Aphrodite are the sub-
jects of a very melodramatic scene in a famous
passage of the *Odyssey.* In brief, only Apollo,
Athena, and Poseidon are respectfully handled
by the Homeric poems. Gladstone summed
up the matter strikingly, when he said that

none of Homer's gods was as good as the swine-herd Eumæus.

Such unedifying stories aroused the pro-tests of the philosophers beginning with Xen-ophanes and culminating with Plato, who ex-cluded Homer from his ideal State. Later still, the Church Fathers, beginning with Tertullian, were zealous in quoting immoral passages in their denunciation of paganism. Of course the blend of religious ideas of the indigenous Medi-terraneans and the invading Hellenes from the North explains many of these incongruities. The nearer the Olympians approach the old Mediterranean nature gods, the more reverend do they become. We smile at the lame smith of the gods puffing through the halls of Olympus as he pours wine for the immortals, but we find Hephæstus, the old fire deity, a truly majestic figure when in combat with the river-god Xanthus. The higher gods are no longer merely nature's powers, like the person-alities of the Vedas. Zeus, whose name and cult show survivals of early animistic concep-tions of the divine sky—for he is cloud-gath-erer, thunderer, hurler of the lightning, and lord of the storm-wind—is something more than this in Homer. Nor is Apollo any longer the sun, nor Artemis the moon. These and all the others were personalities as real to the old Greeks as Jesus or Mary are to Christians. A few of the inferior divinities or dæmons, the nymphs, fauns, river-gods, wind-gods, remained pure nature powers, and some of them never became fully anthropomorphic even at a later time. However, despite the levity displayed in some parts of the Homeric poems, scenes fabricated chiefly by the minstrels whose business it was to amuse, we must add that the deeper utterances show us grand and sublime concepts of the gods. Especially is this true of Zeus, who, though jealous and revengeful like Jahveh, is still a god of righteousness and pity in his dealings with men. In the opening lines of the *Odyssey*, it is not the gods, but the wickedness of men themselves which is said to bring evil on earth.

The Homeric system, while it tells us much about theology and ritual, gives us only a faint idea of eschatology. If we except certain late additions to the poems, we find that they are little concerned with the life of the soul hereafter, and tell us nothing of the cult of the dead nor the need of propitiating ghosts. But we know that the Greeks from very early times believed, as all primitive peoples do, that each man had a soul which inhabited the body as its life-spirit, and that this soul survived the dissolution of the body, and either departed to a shadowy realm where it passed a mournful existence, or still hovered about the tomb. In either case it needed offerings from surviving relatives, and if proper burial rites were not performed, it was able to harm the living. Hence, throughout the history of Greek warfare, enemies as well as allies were scrupulously buried, and a truceless war, in which no opportunity was given for the burial of the dead, was regarded as utterly impious. The tombs excavated by Schliemann at Mycenæ were found provided with objects of gold and silver, which show that the soul was believed to live almost the same life hereafter that it had lived on earth. Gradually the worship of the dead grew, and a special class of the dead so deified became heroes, an idea which was later to assume great proportions. The fear of the ghost-world seems to have grown strong by the seventh century B. C., and we have a reflection of it in the later strata of the *Odyssey*, especially in the *Necyia* or *Descent into Hell* of Odysseus in the eleventh book, and in a scene copied from it at the opening of the last book, where the dead suitors of Penelope are escorted down the dank ways by Hermes.

The *Necyia,* the most striking episode in the poems, seems to have little in common with the Homeric picture of religion, but rather to be a recrudescence of earlier beliefs. Wilhelm Christ believed it was influenced by Egyptian ideas. The catalogue of famous women seems to be the composition of a bard of the Hesiodic school. The picture of Hades, which Odysseus, seated at the trench without, did not enter, and especially the description of retributive punishments meted out by Minos to certain great sinners—Tantalus, Tityus, and Sisyphus—are quite out of harmony with the Homeric spirit, which does not reward good men nor punish bad ones. The last lines have been ascribed to late rhapsodists, perhaps rightly to Onomacritus, the poet of the court of Pisistratus, who, in the belief of Wilamowitz, took the scenes from Orphism, which taught that only initiated and purified souls could escape the torments of Hell.

The *Necyia* paints in gloomy hues the realm of king Hades and his queen Persephone. Ever afterwards the awfulness of death gath-

ered around these rulers of the shades, who
alone of all the gods were implacable, and
whose favor could be invoked by mortals only
to wreak vengeance on enemies. Homer's picture of life is cheerless and melancholy, but is
far preferable to death, which was regarded as
the worst of all fates. If man were merely the
"plaything of the gods," as Plato expresses it,
there was no hope that his wrongs would be
righted hereafter, and no promise of reward
was held out to him who had lived a righteous
life. As Gruppe has said: "Behind the woe
in which he thinks he lives, the Homeric Greek
sees a greater, never-ending woe threatening
him in the future." [4] For of all the fancies con-
jured up by the fears of men about their future state none is more hopeless than that de-
picted here. Erebus, the realm of king Hades,
lies on the western side of Ocean in the land of
the Cimmerians who dwelt in mist—its entrance amid the poplar and willow groves of
Persephone. Tartarus, the prototype of Mil-
ton's Hell, is a gloomy abyss beneath the earth
where rebel Titans are imprisoned. The Ely-
sian Fields are only mentioned once in the
poems as the germ of the later Isles of the
Blessed, which were not definitely conceived

until the time of Hesiod. The mead of aspho-
del, upon which the shadowy spirits tread, is
frequently mentioned. The gray leaves and
yellow blossoms of this plant were, perhaps,
symbolic of the pallor of death and gloom of
the underworld. It was commonly planted on
Greek graves and later was connected with the
cult of Persephone. Homer's heroes, good and
bad alike, are sent to this cheerless abode,
where their existence is even more terrible than
their dwelling-place.

Rohde remarks that it is wrong to speak of a
future life at all in Homer's account, for the
spirits lead only a shadowy copy of their life
on earth, one nearly as neutral as Sheol.
Charon, the ferryman, is not mentioned, nor
the river Lethe. The "brazen-voiced hound of
Hades," fifty-headed, relentless, and strong,
first appears in Hesiod. The "down-flowing
water of the Styx, the greatest and most dread
oath for the blessed gods," is mentioned only
twice. The one ray of light in this dismal
state is that it is not everlasting, since Odysseus sees no ghost older than the second or
third generation before his time. Pindar's account of the dead entertaining themselves
with horse races and athletic sports, with games

of dice and music of the harp, has no counterpart here. The ghost-world had gradually im-
proved by his day. The very utterance of the
"strengthless heads of the dead" is only an in-
articulate squeak, which the poet compares
with the gibbering of bats. Their spectral
forms, bereft of bone and sinew, "sweep
shadow-like around," and all, except the old
Theban seer Tiresias, have forgotten their
earthly existence, and can be recalled to mo-
mentary consciousness only by drinking the
blood of the victim slain by Odysseus. Here
there is neither rest nor peace, joy nor happiness. Amid such gruesome surroundings
Achilles could well answer Odysseus' praise for
his former renown with these words: "Nay,
speak not comfortably to me of death, oh great
Odysseus. Rather would I live on ground as
the hireling of another, with a landless man
who had no great livelihood, than bear sway
among all the dead that be departed." [5]

It is no wonder, then, that the drab features
of such an existence should have called forth
protests which proclaimed a definite hope of
future happiness and a less definite fear of future misery. The strife for existence was hard.
Hesiod must have echoed the groans of many

a wretched wight when he sang: "The earth is full of ills, of ills the sea." It was a time when men were ready for a more hopeful view of the future life, a view which would promise them a tolerable existence beyond, which had been denied them here. It was in the sixth century that such ideas began to find expression in the teachings of the Orphics—a sect named after the legendary minstrel of Thrace to whom the new ideas were ascribed—and in certain other voluntary and mystical societies, such as the one centered at Eleusis, in whose splendid rites the better elements of Greek religion were intensified. These were naturally connected not with the deities of the sky, but with those of the earth and the world below.

The doctrines of Orphism, based largely on Hesiod and his successors, with its initiatory rites adopted from Phrygia and Crete, spread over the Greek world like a wave of reform. Here was taught a very different kind of hereafter from that pictured by Homer. With Homer life on earth, however hard and sombre, was nevertheless preferable to death. To the Orphics, however, existence in the body was not life, but a living death, and what we call death was the door of freedom for the soul

[27]

from its prison-house. The true life is the one to come, when the soul has regained its former communion with the gods, for the soul was regarded as celestial both in its nature and origin. So immortality became a moral motive, and sin on this earth must be punished and the righteous rewarded. This new conception of judgment, of penalties and rewards according to the way in which one had lived, was taken over by Pindar and Æschylus. Two things were bequeathed by Orphism, not only to later Greek religion, but to religion in general: the doctrine of the divine nature of man, *i. e.*, immortality from the beginning, and the practice of personal holiness.

The most pan-Hellenic of the Greek mysteries were those celebrated from very early times at the village of Eleusis near Athens, at first in honor of Pluto, Demeter, and Persephone; later in honor of Dionysus, who replaced the god of the lower world. Although for a long time these mysteries formed an unauthorized and unofficial cult, by the fifth century B. C. they had become a recognized part of the Athenian public worship. Their adoption marks the first opportunity for a Greek to think apart from the traditional religion. They were open to all Athenians and to all Greeks "of intelligible speech and pure of blood." Later on they were open to slaves, to women, and finally to non-Hellenes, only traitors, murderers, and sacrilegious persons being excluded. Thus they became as truly national and international as the Olympic games or the Delphic oracle, and endured all through paganism down to the advent of Christianity. In short, the Eleusinian mysteries formed the first world-religion in Europe. As the doctrines were secretly taught and the initiates were bound to disclose nothing seen or heard, we really know but little about them. But we do know that their aim was ritualistic purity, and we infer something more, that they inculcated a higher belief in the immortality of the soul than was taught elsewhere in the ancient world. Both Pindar and Sophocles were initiates, and in guarded language they speak of the future blessedness of those who were inducted.[6] It was through the influence of these mysteries that Athens also came to evolve higher views of an after-life than were pictured by Homer. Thus, death could be

[29]

imagined by Socrates as either a dreamless sleep or, in some wise, a preparation for a higher life.

During the centuries of Athens' glory perhaps the most impressive characteristics of Greek religion were beauty and joy—the pomp of public worship, the beautiful temples, artistic cult-statues, stately processions, joyous festivals, and solemn ritual. In all this we see reflected the character of a people endowed beyond all others with a sense of the beautiful and the capacity to enjoy life, a people who worshipped gods in whom they saw their own ideals. Only consider that most brilliant worship with which Athena was honored by her people, the great Panathenaic procession, which lives again for us in the beautiful frieze of the Parthenon. Surely no deity was ever worshipped more gloriously than was the virgin goddess by such a galaxy of lovely forms moving majestically along with their wealth of color in the luminous atmosphere of the city of the violet crown and amid the immortal monuments of those immortal men.

But beauty was only one feature of Greek worship. Another as prominent was joyousness. Greek religion rested lightly on men.

The central characteristic of Greek mythology was that it largely freed men from the domination of fear. Piety, as we have seen, was merely a civic duty. The Greek, unlike the Hebrew, never judged his conduct by stern standards. He was not impressed by any deep sense of sin, nor did he have much idea of the loving care of the gods. He thought rather well of himself and not too well of his human gods. If he only avoided the great moral crimes and did not arouse the "envy of the gods" by transgressing the limits set for human ambition, he had little to fear. For it was deeply ingrained in the Greek consciousness that—to use a phrase from Herodotus—"the god suffers none but himself to be proud." Nemesis, the power which "scourges pride and scorn," was sure to overtake the man who overstepped. The Greek realized how arbitrary the future was and reflected on the fact that the wicked were as likely to prosper as the good. Out of such reflection had grown not only respect for the powers which could cause prosperity and adversity at will, but also the desire to win their future favors by sacrifice and prayer, and to thank them for the past. The recurring festivals, celebrated with pro-

cessions and music, and accompanied by theat-
rical, orchestral, or gymnastic competitions,
were real holidays. Athens observed as many
holidays during the year, as we do Sundays.
Even when the opening days of certain festivals
were sad, they always ended joyously. Thus,
the beginning of the Spartan *Hyacinthia,* an old
nature festival, was connected with grief at the
death of vegetation, but it ended with joy for
the coming harvest and confidence in a re-
awakening of nature, as was shown by its procession of boys and girls with harps and flutes
to the temple of Apollo. Men felt that the gods
could be made to become interested in them
and so strove for their help and protection.

But amid the beauty and joy of Greek worship we must not close our eyes to the fact that
it also had a darker side, even if we meet that
side least in Greek literature and art. Calami-
ties came and were ascribed to malevolent or
offended deities. Criminals then, as now, were
followed by the Furies, the avenging twinges
of conscience. Repulsive features were also
present side by side with nobler ones, and not
all of these were survivals of earlier days.
Philosophers and poets were constantly de-
nouncing immoral myths, and some cults were

characterized by orgiastic rites. But, on the whole, Greek worship was pure and refined. Sex-defilement was rare in the temples, and there certainly was no licentiousness in the sacred marriage drama at Eleusis, in spite of the insinuations of the early Church Fathers, who had a special interest in emphasizing the crudest and worst elements in Græco-Roman worship. Aphrodite's cult, in general, was decorous and her statues were almost uniformly draped down to the time of Praxiteles. Hellenistic artists were often fond of displaying her charms with realistic effect, but such works were no more related to the real religion of the Greeks than are Rubens' voluptuous Magdalenes to real Christianity. Temple prostitution in Aphrodite's honor was mostly late or found among the Asiatic Greeks, and was confined to only a few places, such as Corinth and Cyprus. Phallic ritual, although freely used in vegetation cults, was rarely obscene. Thus ugliness, while it did exist in Greek worship, was never prominent.

With the freedom and formalism of Greek religion, some have questioned whether the Greeks after all were really religious. But if religion means the consciousness of weakness

and dependence on a power or powers higher
than mortals, and if it is a longing for sympathy
and protection from the powers which control
the world of nature, and if prayer and sacrifice are religious acts, the Greeks were certainly
a deeply religious people. Nestor's son Pisistratus tells Telemachus at Pylus that "all men
stand in need of the gods," a verse which
Melanchthon regarded as the most beautiful in
Homer. Thales, by the beginning of the sixth
century B. C., said "all things are full of the
gods." Clearchus, in the *Anabasis* [7] of Xenophon, tells the arch-traitor Tissaphernes that
"all things in all places are subject to the gods,
and all alike the gods hold in their control."
Such sentiments disclose the universality of
religious feeling among the Greeks. The material of religion, in its two branches of theology
and ritual, was much the same in Greece as
elsewhere—sacrifice, prayer and hymn, rites
of propitiation and thanksgiving, purification
and expiation, belief in dæmons and ghosts
of the departed, in magic, in ancestor worship,
and divination. Such elements form the common stock of all religions, and may be found
even in Christianity itself. What was peculiar
to the Greek, then, was not the material, but

the way in which it was handled. As one writer has said: "Where the Australian stopped, the Greek passed on." Things of ugliness were refined into things of beauty. Every Greek town had more shrines than a Christian city has churches. Athens alone had over two hundred. You remember how St. Paul, as he saw the city full of idols, chided the Athenians of his day for being "somewhat superstitious." He found altars not only to many gods, but one to an "unknown god," which had been erected there, as elsewhere by ancient pagans to correct any possible oversight, but which with his religious zeal St. Paul immediately identified with the Christian God.

Sacrifice was the sign of the reverent spirit. It was made mostly for favors expected rather than for those received. The traffic idea of sacrifice was instinctive in the Greek. Hesiod said that "gifts move the gods and reverent kings." An ancient Greek proverb ran: "Gifts persuade even gods." [8] This was an idea that constantly met the denunciation of the philosophers. Thus, Plato said it reduced worship to an act of merchandise between gods and men, and he protested that God could not be "seduced by presents like a villainous money-lender." Xenophon tells us that Socrates admired the line of Hesiod which ran: "according to thine ability do sacrifice to the immortal gods," for he believed that "the joy of the gods is greater in proportion to the holiness of the giver." [9] Euripides also declared that "he who with pious heart doth sacrifice, small though the offering be, salvation wins." [10] Votive offerings for favors received were to be found in every temple, so that many temples were veritable museums of works of art. Apollo's shrine on Delos alone is said to have possessed sixteen hundred gold and silver bowls.

Prayer was also a universal phenomenon of Greek religion, following Homer's sentiment that "from the gods come all good things." Prayers for success were offered by armies before battle, by farmers for crops, by athletes for victory, by hunters, in short by every one. Every symposium began and ended with prayer, and political assemblies, as still often to-day, were regularly opened with it. Pericles is said to have commenced every speech with the prayer that he might "utter no unfitting word." Plato in the Timæus says that at the beginning of every undertaking, whether great or small, "all who participate in virtue, to the least degree, invariably invoke a god." Men prayed to Demeter for crops, to Dionysus for their vineyards, to Asclepius for health, to Apollo, Hermes, or Pan for their flocks, and, if desirous of foreknowledge, to Apollo, who in one sense was mightier than Zeus. For Louis Dyer has rightly remarked that "Zeus was a king among gods, who reigned, but governed not. His Premier was the Delphic god." Women prayed especially to Demeter and Persephone. The gods were invoked at births and weddings.

The same traffic idea was present in prayer as in sacrifice. While in Homer prayers seldom expressed thanksgiving, but were rather petitions spontaneously rising to the lips in seasons of stress, they later changed their character, and so evoked the same protest as sacrifice. Xenophanes urged men "to pray for power to do that which is right." Xenophon records that Socrates' ideal was "to pray for that which is good, without further specification, believing the gods best know what is good." In the *Second Alcibiades* Plato has Socrates approve this old Spartan prayer: "Give us, O King Zeus, what is good, whether we pray for it or not, and avert from us the evil, even if we pray for it." Socrates' ideal of prayer is contained in the beautiful one to Pan, which occurs at the end of the *Phædrus:* "O beloved Pan, and all ye other gods of this place, grant to me that I be made beautiful in my soul within, and that all external possessions be in harmony with my inner man. May I consider the wise man rich; and may I have such wealth as only the self-restrained man can bear or endure." He then turns to Phædrus and asks: "Do we need anything more, Phædrus? For me that prayer is enough." [11]

Thus we have seen that religion entered deeply into the lives of the Greeks, and was constantly before them in nearly every event in the lives of states and individuals, for on the favor of the gods hung the prosperity of both. The Greek calendar was merely an invention to determine the festivals. Greek religious imagination constantly tended to inspire Greek art, both plastic and literary, and philosophy. Greek art was only the handmaid of religion and would have satisfied even the definition of Tolstoi. Beautiful sculptures have preserved to our eyes the very forms of the Greek gods which were present to the Greek imagination at different times. Vase-paintings tell us of the ritual and externals of worship. Temple ruins let our imaginations restore the grandeur of their holy places. And as for Greek literature, despite the absence of sacred books, it fairly teems with religious thought and sentiment. The Greek drama was religious in its origin and remained so throughout its development. Greek philosophy was always theological. Greek law was religious in its origin and evolution. Even the great public games, such as those at Olympia and Delphi, were religious meetings, at first associated with the worship of heroes, later with that of gods. They figured among the strongest Pan-hellenic influences which were constantly making for nationality and for a broader religion than that of tribe or city. Great poets, thinkers, and artists found much more to praise than to condemn in the simple popular faith. Pindar and Sophocles, Phidias and Praxiteles, were religious men. Aristotle, in his day, could say that the word "father" when applied to Zeus included the idea of his care for men. This idea first appears in Greek literature in a passage of Plato's *Apology,* in which Socrates says to his judges that "no evil can come to a good man either in life or after death, and God does not neglect him." St. Paul could quote the sentiment of the late Greek poet Aratus that "we are his offspring." And the Stoic Cleanthes, in his hymn to the majesty of Zeus, could say much the same thing, even though he meant thereby that human reason is a fragment of the divine. The human quality of the gods and the divine nature of man have never been apprehended more clearly than by the Greeks. While the Hebrews taught that men were fashioned in the image of God, the Greeks fashioned their Gods in the image of men. It was Heraclitus who said that "mortals are immortals and immortals are mortals, living the immortals' death and dying the immortals' life" [12]—perhaps enigmatically referring to the Orphic conception of the body as the prison of the soul, from which the soul escapes at death, in order to enter upon its real existence.

II. THE INFLUENCE OF GREEK RELIGION ON EARLY CHRIS-TIANITY: THE GREEK GODS TURNED SAINTS

IT IS not surprising that this religion, which entered so vitally and deeply into every phase of Greek life for a period of so many centuries, should have left a permanent influence on the beliefs and ritual of Christianity which was destined to supersede it. This influence has affected the conquering faith in many ways, leaving its traces upon the theology, ethics, and rites of the whole Christian Church, and imposing customs, beliefs, and superstitions upon the Eastern Church of the modern Greek people. For *disjecta membra* of the old religion can be found everywhere in the Greece of to-day, the past constantly showing through the present.

The debt of Christianity at large to Greek religion and philosophy is a complex and many-sided question, one to be set forth also in other volumes of the present Series. In general, it

may be said that Greek religion was not ob-
literated by Christianity, but that the two were
fused, and that after the process was com-
pleted many of the older forms and beliefs re-
appeared. To the most casual observer there
is an enormous gulf between the simple appeal
of the Sermon on the Mount, which promul-
gated a new law of conduct without any
metaphysical basis, and the reasoned body of
doctrines found in the Nicene creed, which still
forms the dominant element in Christianity
to-day. While one fits the simple lives of
Palestinian peasants, the other is the result of
the acute speculations of Greek philosophers.
The passing from one to the other carried the
Christian worshiper from a system primarily
interested in conduct to one interested in the
fundamentals of belief.

To understand the transformation by which
Christianity, an oriental faith, gradually became rooted in Hellenism, we must understand
the environment of the Greek world into which
Christianity was to pass from the Jewish atmosphere of Palestine. For centuries Greek
philosophy, always theological in character,
had been concerned not only with the physical
world, but with conduct and the nature of the

god-head. It was inevitable, therefore, that primitive Christianity, if it was to succeed among educated Greeks, should be influenced by Greek ways of thinking and that its theology should be recast in a Greek mold. Christianity came into ground that was prepared to receive it. But, at the same time, by the time of its advent, the elements of Greek education were widely diffused among all classes. This education had long aroused the habit of inquiry which was at the basis of Greek philosophy and which, during the later centuries, had inculcated definite logical and metaphysical methods which were certain to affect the new religion.

We see the influence of Greek philosophy especially in the Christian concept of God and in that of ethics. Greek speculation had long laid down the fundamental attributes of Deity, its oneness, personality, and benevolence. The primitive Christian belief in one God, creator of the world and kindly Father of men, rested on the naïve conviction of a spiritual revelation. Greek philosophy was to strengthen this conviction with a reasoned, intellectual basis. The Greeks in their gradual ascent from animism to Olympus had finally evolved the belief in the personality of the godhead. As

[43]

the human mind was the real self, so the great mind behind or within nature was essentially personal, the creator and moral governor of the world. Furthermore, God was an absolute Being and this complex idea was destined to change the simple Christian conception, since the essence of God had to be defined. So the Christian God became more metaphysical and less spiritual, and much of the primitive faith, which had been based on the simple love of God and trust in Jesus, was lost.

On its ethical side also Christianity was to be influenced no less vitally. The Jews had always been more interested in problems of life than in disputes about the nature of God. Hebrew philosophy had never become systematized, but had remained in the antithetical and proverbial stage. Through the influence of Greek thought, the primitive Christian ethics were to become speculative and mystical. Moral conduct and discipline were quite as much the aim of the later systems of Greek philosophy as they were of Christianity, although each approached the problem differently. To the Christian, morality rested upon the Jewish theocratic idea of a divine command, but the Greeks had long been seeking an independent origin consonant with natural law. To the one, infraction of the moral code was sin and demanded repentance and forgiveness, as the means of restoration to grace; to the other it meant failure; while forgiveness was difficult, redemption could be secured by appropriate ceremonies of purgation which quieted the conscience. Christian morality became subordinate to belief and consequently declined from its original stern standards. The ethics of the Sermon on the Mount, which had conquered by its simple sincerity, later came into conflict with the ethics of Roman law, which was a fusion of Roman legal ideas of human rights and the concept of human relationships as taught by the Stoic philosophers. It was Greek religion, however, rather than philosophy, which influenced the ceremonial of the Church by the spell of the elaborate rituals of the Greek mysteries celebrated at Eleusis and elsewhere in the Eastern part of the Roman Empire. Since these old mystic associations had practically the same aim as Christianity—the love of a purer faith and life, and the inculcation of the spirit of brotherhood—the two systems were bound to be drawn together. We see this process of as-

similation especially in the ritual of the two
great sacraments of the early Church—Baptism and the Lord's Supper—practices symbolic
of entrance into the new kingdom and membership in the new society. At first the simple
baptism of water followed immediately on con-
version and without the need of a special
minister; a little later it was preceded by
fasting and brief instruction on the significance
of the rite. But soon the very name and concept of this primitive ritual were changed. By
the time of Justin Martyr it was known as the
"Enlightenment," and a little later, by that of
Tertullian, it was called the "Seal," names
which were taken directly from the Greek
mysteries. It was carried out with a mystic
formula whose technical terminology was
taken from the same source. It was performed
in secret and at stated times and in the great
churches and only after a long preparation.
Similarly the Eucharist, which commemorated
Jesus' last meal with his disciples, at first consisted merely of a blessing on the wine and
broken bread, followed by the converted par-
taking of both immediately after baptism and
then by prayers of thanksgiving and supplication. But by the middle of the second century

[46]

the holy table was known as the altar, the offerings laid upon it were conceived as mysteries, and the priest officiated in secret. Thus, under the influence of the old Greek mysteries, the whole concept of original Christian worship was changed, and throughout the East the simple rites were metamorphosed into a rich and varied ceremonial carried out amid the glare of lights with processions of torch-bearers chanting hymns, the central rite being hidden from the public.

Apart from these more general influences, an even more definite one can be traced in the Eastern Church in the continued persistence of many other old Greek rites, beliefs, and superstitions, which live even to-day under cover of Christianity. It is with these survivals of Greek religion rather than with influences of Greek speculation that we are here concerned.

The living Greek has inherited not only the lands, the language, and, to some extent, the blood and character of the old Greeks, but also many traditions and beliefs from the ancient religion. As Edmond About has said in his *Memoire sur Égine:* "Of all the ruins of Greece, the Greek people is not the least inter-

esting." Here he has piquantly expressed a
real fact—the survival of customs and characteristics of the old Greeks. Thus the Romaic
speech, despite increments from Turkish,
Arabic, Italian, Albanian, Frank, and Slavic
sources, is, after all, merely the survival of
Byzantine Greek, which, in turn, was descended from the *koiné* or patois in use everywhere in the eastern Mediterranean lands after
the conquests of Alexander. In spite of all the
political vicissitudes of the Greek people, their
language has resisted all invaders. Fallmer-
ayer's belief, enunciated many years ago and
even now applauded by certain propagandists,
that the mainland Greeks of his day had no
claim to Hellenic descent, but had been replaced by Slavic blood during the great Slavic
immigrations into Greece from the sixth to the
end of the tenth centuries, has long since been
abandoned in most quarters. Slavic influence
certainly can be traced in the physical characteristics of the Greek people, but the few Slavic
speech-forms now found in Romaic are not survivals of the far off days when Slavic hordes
overran the Balkan peninsula, but rather are
borrowings through Turkish and Albanian, in
which languages Slavic words are still plenti-

ful. With certain reservations, then, the modern Greeks may be said to be descended from the Greeks of antiquity. No one who has a first-hand, even though superficial, knowledge of the present-day Greeks can fail to have remarked how the old Greek character—its alertness and sobriety, its activity and curiosity, its intelligence and taste for politics—everywhere reappears. A more extended and intimate acquaintance with their customs, traditions, and superstitions will show that these also are largely descended from older ones. Nowhere is this connection with the past more noticeable than in the religious survivals, the main subject of the present sketch, which will show that antiquity still vitally influences the present. In short, all phases of the modern life of the Greek people are affected by an unconscious, and at times quite conscious, effort to keep up older traditions. In language, blood, character, traditions, and religious beliefs, there has been fusion in Greece throughout the ages, but still the chief element in them all is Greek.

For the first three centuries, down to the time of Constantine, Christianity had to fight for its very existence. At first it was known as a "pernicious superstition" of the Jews,

[49]

whose votaries Tacitus termed "haters of the human race." Its exclusiveness and intolerance aroused the animosity of Rome, which was tolerant toward all sects. Its membership was drawn from the humblest ranks and consisted largely of women. As it spread, it grew more intolerant of other creeds than Judaism itself, and hence came to be looked upon as a specially vicious branch of the latter and hostile to the peace of the Empire. Its first persecution under Nero was, therefore, more political than religious in character. In the early part of the second century Trajan declared it illegal and its members were liable to death, although the emperor's correspondence with the provincial governor Pliny shows that so severe a sentence was rarely carried out. Consequently the persecutions under Trajan were local and popular rather than general and fostered by the government. By the third century, however, the Church counted converts in palace and at court. Decline in prosperity and anarchy in government during that terrible century naturally turned men's minds to this religion of promise and peace, and the trend of political events, despite the persecution under Decius, favored its ultimate victory the following century. The Church was now tolerated, even if it was "a vast, organized defiance of law." At the end of the third century the struggle between the Church and State entered its last stage, for under Diocletian the Church had its last persecution. It had now grown too strong to be successfully persecuted. At the opening of the fourth century Constantine was shrewd enough to see the advantages to himself in his civil wars of an alliance with the Church. By the edict of toleration signed at Milan by Constantine and his colleague Licinius in 313, following that of Galerius in 311 which had permitted the Christians to practice their religion "if they did nothing contrary to good order," Christianity became the favored religion of the court, and civil advancement was only possible through its ranks. It was only a step to the edict of Theodosius toward the close of the century by which it became the recognized religion of the state. This change in its fortunes was the chief event of that century, for, though less than one-tenth of the population of the Empire was enrolled as Christian, it was by far the most important element in that population, since it was completely organized and was massed in the urban communities.

As victor the Church adopted the only reasonable policy—to adapt itself to existing conditions so far as this was not opposed to its fundamental principles. It adopted, in fact, the same policy in the Græco-Roman world that it employed everywhere else—the enlisting in its service of everything in existing beliefs and practices which it found useful. It would have been surprising if, while trying to propagate its doctrines in the Roman Empire, the Church had repudiated all that theretofore had served to express religious feeling. Paganism here was to react strongly on Christianity, and the latter found it advantageous to enter upon a policy of conciliation and, at times, even of compromise by assimilating and blending older ideas with its own. Some investigators, such as Delehaye, may have underestimated this policy of compromise, while others, such as Lawson, may have exaggerated it. But that there was such a policy needs but little proof, for it was the only logical one for the Church to follow. This policy is largely responsible for the survival of old rites and beliefs among the masses of the people in the Eastern Church. The pagan Empire gradually became Christian; at the same time the Christian Church became largely pagan. Later on, when the Church penetrated barbarian Germany, there was a similar reaction, although there it more easily got rid of ancient beliefs and practices. There, as in the Græco-Roman world, the advantages to the Church outweighed any possible loss.

ᴷ The Greeks and Romans were ready from the first to admit Christ into their pantheons of gods, since both peoples were tolerant of foreign cults. Tertullian, the earliest of the Latin Fathers, tells us that Tiberius proposed to apotheosize Christ, though the statement is now generally discredited. The historian Lampridius says that both Hadrian and Severus Alexander had in mind the building of a temple in honor of Christ, and that the latter placed in his private chapel statues of Christ and Abraham along with those of Orpheus and Apollonius of Tyana. St. Augustine records that Homer, Pythagoras, Christ, and Paul were worshipped together in his time. ᴧ But the Greeks, while willing to accept new gods, were not so willing to discard their old ones. Christianity could ridicule these gods by pointing out their licentious character and cruelty; but it could not get rid of them. It was not so difficult to drive out the chief Olympians, as these stood relatively aloof from the practical affairs of life and consequently could be alienated more easily from the popular allegiance. Moreover, their worship had gradually become formal and ceremonial. It was a much harder task to get rid of the chthonian deities, since their gifts of healing had brought them very close to men, and consequently paganism was destined to fight its last battles in the temples of such gods as Asclepius and Serapis. But the hardest task of all was to drive out the lesser divinities or "potencies," which early Christian writers still called by their old name "dæmons." These had been intimately connected for many centuries with every phase of life and were destined to survive the victory of Christianity, for belief in them was ingrained in the very nature of the people. The Greeks were tolerant and, therefore, hostile to the intolerance of the new faith. This very intolerance was to prove the greatest obstacle to the progress of Christianity. Despite imperial edicts little progress would

have been possible, if the Church Fathers had
not seen the necessity of preaching conciliation.
The masses of the people in both Greece and
Italy were incurably polytheistic by nature;
although they might conform outwardly with
the new religion, they persisted in retaining
many of their old beliefs. It is doubtful if they
really felt any antagonism between the old and
the new, for they willingly worshipped both.
The Church had to meet these conditions and
ultimately tolerated the retention of many beliefs and practices, even when it did not sanc-
tion them. It had to leave to the slow opera-
tion of time the healing of differences.

The people continued, doubtless, to worship at their accustomed places. Christian
churches were sure to replace pagan temples
or to be erected on ancient holy spots. Christ,
Mary, and the Saints gradually replaced the
old deities. Sometimes saints whose names
and attributes were similar to those of the dispossessed gods were given to the churches, and
Christian festivals continued to be held on the
dates of pagan ones. Only gradually did the
Church learn that such concessions brought
evil in their train and that the old beliefs could
not be eradicated. Church Fathers, such as

St. Chrysostom, remonstrated in vain against the retention of the older practices. In spite of its intention, then, the Church was destined to become colored by polytheism, the old deities being perpetuated under the guise of Christian adaptation. The people were taught that the saints were not to be worshipped like Christ and Mary, but that they were merely mediators between God and men; but the people, polytheistic in their nature, were sure to regard them as they regarded Christ, the great mediator. Gradually the provinces of activity of the Christian saints were sharply defined, just as had been the case with the old deities. In course of time the saints usurped the allegiance of men's minds, even obscuring the persons of the Trinity. The powers of the Deity were thus delegated to a host of these saints, who were believed to be nearer to men and easier of access. Thus, in a certain sense, it is true that the deities of the Homeric pantheon were replaced by Christian saints.

The Eastern Church to-day shows the result of its early policy of conciliation and compromise. Its members are devoted to the Christian Trinity, but in a very true sense they still remain largely pagan. Although they make the sign of the cross as frequently as their Roman cousins do, and although they believe in the miraculous powers of the saints and their icons and observe their festivals, the Greek people are still polytheistic and pagan in temperament. They still believe in the old idea of sacrifice and in divination by omens, dreams, and even oracles. They believe in a great number of supernatural beings who are quite outside the pale of Christianity. While some of these beings are more or less disguised under Christian beliefs, others live on almost unchanged. Especially is this polytheistic background true of the common people. They, like the Greeks of old, still live in a world peopled by such spirits, to some of whom they pray and sacrifice for favors, and from others of whom they protect themselves by exorcisms and magic rites. Such beings are far from imaginary, for the people believe that they can be seen, heard, and, at times, even touched.

Christianity, then, is only a part of the religion of the ordinary Greek. Externally he is a Christian; but deep in his own consciousness he is still a pagan. The priest, often as ignorant as his flock, does not try to interpret this mixture of pagan tradition and Christian rites, for he neither feels nor understands it. Consequently the people are never taught to feel any contrast in their mixed ideas of the godhead and continue to pray and sacrifice both to pagan spirits and to the Christian God. Although they give their main allegiance to the persons of the Trinity and to Mary, after all, as Sir James Rennell Rodd has said, they believe more in the old Fates than in God and more in the Homeric Hades than in the Christian hereafter. Many of the present-day survivals, such as belief in the Evil Eye and in certain forms of magic, go back to the earliest and most primitive notions, even to a time before the fusion of Mediterranean and Hellenic ideas which produced the religion of the historical Greeks. Still others, such as belief in revenants, while Greek in origin, have been largely influenced by alien peoples who have come into contact with the Greeks since antiquity. The study of such survivals is a fascinating one, but it must be pursued with caution; for we must be constantly on our guard lest we confuse genuine survivals from antiquity with scholastic interpolations of recent times, the result of modern education and intercourse. The folk-songs and especially the folk-tales which one sometimes hears to-day are certainly not always the result of pure tradition. Thus the present-day stories about Alexander the Great are largely the result of imagination, which has obscured the ancient tradition.

One of the chief charms of travel in Greek lands to-day is meeting with these survivals of old customs and beliefs. On many an isolated island and in many a remote valley of the mainland, where there has been small contact with the outside world, the peasants will be found to have preserved not only the speech, but the superstitions and customs of the Old World. These are to be met with in every phase and detail of domestic life. We find them in the agricultural and pastoral life of the people, in their industries and medical lore, in their games and dances, and especially in the host of ceremonies connected with births, marriages, and death. These survivals, so interesting to traveler and folklorist, are gradually disappearing with the increased facilities of communication and extension of education. Only here and there and generally under difficulties can they still be traced. Sometimes a religious survival may be confined to a single

folk-tale or folk-song. And it will not be long
before such survivals will have disappeared almost completely. But we are fortunate in having many collections of such songs and tales,
which have been made from the time of Leo
Allatius, the Chiote theologian and folklorist
of the early seventeenth century, down to our
own day. The list of such collections com-
prises many distinguished names of French,
German, English, and Greek scholars,—Fauriel
and Legrand, Passow, Schmidt, and von Hahn,
Abbott and Garnett, Polites, Zampelios, and a
host of local Greek historians.

Before discussing the complicated question
of whether the Christian saints have succeeded
to the old deities, we shall briefly discuss the
Christian use of temple sites, and then mention
a few of the survivals of the major gods which
exist in folklore,—chiefly of Zeus, Poseidon,
Demeter, Artemis, Aphrodite, Apollo and the
woodland Pan. Delehaye is probably right in
his belief that it became possible to establish
churches on old temple sites only after the triumph of Christianity, and not in the early centuries of conflict. Christianity certainly did
not wait for the abandonment of such sites before erecting basilicas on ground that had not

been holy. Some time ago Petit de Julle-
ville [13] attempted to trace, through epithets
and sites of Greek churches, a connection between such churches and the old temples. But
many of his deductions were certainly far-
fetched. Thus he connected the Church of the
Twelve Apostles at Athens with the altars of
the twelve gods which are believed to have been
located in the same neighborhood. Consequently only a few examples of the transformation of temples into churches may be regarded
as certain. The best example, of course, is
the Parthenon, whose virgin goddess Athena
was replaced at some unknown date between
the middle of the fifth and middle of the sixth
centuries by the virgin mother of Christ. The
so-called Theseum at Athens was dedicated to
the warrior St. George of Cappadocia. The
church of the Panaghia Blastiké—Virgin of
Fecundity—certainly stands near an old shrine
of Ilithyia, the goddess of fecundity. A church
of St. Nicolas is on the site of a shrine of Poseidon, his prototype. Other examples may be
cited outside Athens, such as the Church of the
Annunciation on Tenos, which was built a century ago on the site of an older one, which in
turn replaced a temple of Poseidon. Within

its precincts is a holy spring with healing powers, and we know that Poseidon was worshipped here as "the Healer." Similarly, holy
caves and groves became sacred spots of Christianity. Thus on the north side of Colonus
near Athens there were visible until recently
the remains of a church in honor of the "safe
saints," a title which is reminiscent of the
Eumenides who had a grove here; and nearby
is a chapel of St. Nicolas, where Poseidon once
had a sanctuary.

Turning next to the survivals of the major
gods in the popular beliefs of to-day we find
only a few that can be called authentic. Most
of these refer to Zeus, who in the old Olympian
system was chief in power and wisdom, and
was, therefore, from the time of Homer onwards frequently known as "the god" or
"God." The word "god," thus used of the
greatest of the immortals, reappears in Romaic
in many compound words where it has the
meaning of "big" or "excessive," that is, like
the gods. It is prefixed to nouns and especially
to adjectives. Thus we have θεόσπιτο, "big
house," θεόκωφος, "stone deaf," and many
similar combinations. In ancient Greek the
same idea was expressed by compounding πᾶν,

"all," with a noun or adjective, as in πάγκαλος, "very beautiful." But more than this, the very name of Zeus survives here and there in place-names. Thus a village at the base of Mount Ida in Crete is still known as Zoulakko, and the top of the sacred Mount Iuktas on the same island is called "Zeus' monument." Bent found the highest hill on the island of Naxos, known in antiquity as the mountain of Milesian Zeus, still called Zia. At the entrance to a cave near its top is an altar—now called the church of Zia—where a priest annually holds a service for the neighboring shepherds, who swear by it their most sacred oath. Schmidt mentions the common Cretan invocation "Divine Zeus, hear me," and says that an oath sworn "by the god of Crete" is still heard in Arachova and Delphi as an expression of wonder.

While most of the powers of Zeus, the descendant of the old Indo-European sky-god, have descended to various saints, Zeus still lives on in the phenomena of nature—thunder, lightning, rain—which are now ascribed to the Christian God. An amatory distich from Crete, which runs, "He that gathereth the clouds, and thundereth, and raineth," recalls

the Homeric epithets of Zeus, "cloud-gatherer,"
"high thunderer," and "rain-bringer." [14] The
thunderbolt, the chief weapon of Zeus, is
known to-day as the "lightning-axe" (ἀστρο-
πελέκι), which is usually, but wrongly, translated as "starry-axe." [15] Axe in this sense
was never used in antiquity, but the Romaic
counterpart is found in the German *"Donner-
keil."* The thunderbolt is sometimes regarded
as the instrument of God's vengeance, as it was
once that of Zeus. Thus Schmidt recounts a
tale which is an echo of the mythical war between the Titans and the Olympians. In it,
giants climb mountains and hurl rocks at God,
just as the Titans piled Pelion on Ossa to scale
Olympus, but God slew them with his bolt even
as did Zeus. One, more courageous than the
rest, tied a bundle of reeds together to reach
heaven, but was burnt to death by the lightning. When his companions attacked again,
most were slain and the rest enclosed in a
mountain, as Enceladus was buried beneath
Ætna. Greek sailors compare the flashes of
lightning with the blows of spears, just as
Aristophanes called lightning the "immortal
lance" of Zeus, and Æschylus spoke of the
god's "sleepless dart." Men, cattle, and even

trees which have been struck by lightning, are
nowadays set apart. In antiquity an altar
would mark a spot thus visited and it became
sacred. Artemidorus tells us that a person so
struck was "excluded from citizenship and honored as a god." Men and cattle struck by
lightning to-day generally do not have to work
thereafter. A peasant crosses himself in passing a tree that has been injured by lightning,
and never takes refuge under it in storm. Certain Romaic phrases remind us rather of Wotan
and Odin than of Zeus, especially those which
represent God as riding, since Zeus never rode.
Thus, when it thunders, one hears that "God
is shoeing his horse," or that "the hoofs of
God's horses are ringing."

The old idea that rain and snow were caused
by Zeus is now transferred to God. The ancient phrase "Zeus rains" is now changed to
"God rains." On Cythera rain-water is called
"God's water," which recalls Theophrastus' as-
cription of it to Zeus. The peasants of the
village of Samos on Cephalonia call a rainy
district "God's sea," and at Arachova in Central Greece the peasants during a drought say,
"Rain, grandfather!" which recalls the old
Athenian rain-prayer, "Rain, dear Zeus, on the

cornlands of the Athenians and their pastures!" [16]

The place of Poseidon, the god of the sea, who dwelt "in his famous palace in the deeps of the mere, his glistening mansions builded, imperishable for ever," is now taken either by St. Nicolas or certain female divinities. But, curiously, one folk-tale from Zante, known as "Captain Thirteen," recalls the lord of the sea and his trident, though even this has been suspected as not being a genuine tradition. Schmidt has found either Poseidon or Nereus represented in folklore as half-human and half-fish riding upon a dolphin, and in a car propelled by dolphins, and so rich—since he owns everything that has been lost in the sea— that he sleeps on a couch of gold. Poseidon's power to cause earthquakes with the stroke of his trident is now transferred to God on Zante, where he causes such disturbances by "shaking his locks," even as did Zeus in the Iliad.

Only meagre traces of the legend or cult of Demeter and Persephone, and these intermixed with Christian elements, are to be found in Greece. In general, as we shall see later, Demeter has been superseded by St. Demetrius, the patron of agriculture and friend of marriage. In 1860 Lenormant [17] heard from an aged Albanian priest at the village of Eleusis a legend about a St. Demetra, who was known there until recent years, many details of which, mixed with Christian and Turkish ideas, remind us of the rape of Persephone by Pluto and Demeter's search for her daughter as related in the old Homeric Hymn. At the base of this story the four chief characters of the ancient version are clearly recognizable,— Demeter, as St. Demetra, Persephone as her daughter, Pluto as a Turkish agha who is in love with the daughter and carries her off to his Epirote castle, and Triptolemus, as the youth who guides the saint in her search, finds the ravisher, and slays him. Even Eleusis appears in the form of Lepsina, and Souli represents the Epirote district of the Acheron.

Vestiges of the legend of Demeter also reappear in other parts of Greece. Thus, around the Arcadian lake of Pheneus, which is drained by an underground channel which later becomes the river Ladon, we find such a trace. It was by this passage, according to a legend preserved by the Augustan grammarian Conon, that Pluto escaped with Persephone. The inhabitants of the present town of Phoniá call this channel the "Devil's Hole," and they believe that when the waters of the lake are high Hades is full and that there will be few deaths in the neighborhood. In still other parts of Greece the peasants speak of a powerful female dæmon who dwells within the mountain, calling her the "Mistress." Thus, in Ætolia, the "Mistress of the world" was found by Lawson to dwell inside a mountain, a beneficent being who gives increase to crops and flocks. The same title is also found in Arcadia, at the village of Pavlitsa, which is on the site of the ancient Phigalia. Pausanias mentions a cave on Mount Elæus near Phigalia, where the "Black Demeter" was honored as the "Mistress." This cave has been identified with one now known as the "Virgin's Gully" in the glen of the Neda just west of the town. Frazer says that the story is current in the neighborhood that the Madonna once took refuge there, shocked by the incestuous love of a brother and sister. This surely recalls the story told by Pausanias and other writers of the retirement to this cave of Demeter, when she was grieved at her brother Poseidon's love for her. Schmidt also found the title "Mistress" in three folk-songs, each of which recounts how the "Mistress" is won in marriage by a mortal lover.

Artemis, the huntress maiden "chaste and fair," has been superseded for the most part by St. Artemidus. But her personality, if not her name, has survived in various localities of Greece. As "Queen of the Mountains" on Cephalonia she leads the Nereids who roam over hill and dale, being taller and fairer than the rest. Just so, in the *Odyssey*, Nausicaa among her maidens is likened to Artemis among her nymphs. In Ætolia we hear of "the lady beautiful," which recalls one of Artemis' titles "Calliste." On Zante she is "the great lady." Whoever has the misfortune to meet her or to speak with her loses sight and voice,—which reminds us of the story of Tiresias, who was blinded for looking upon Athena while she was bathing.

The character and even the name of Aphrodite still survive in a few folk-tales, although St. Catharine and the Fates have taken over most of her functions. In certain tales she appears as "the mother of Eros," and in one of these we read of a wingèd boy with bow and arrows, and of a garden filled with roses, flowers which were once sacred to the goddess of love. In 1858 the Frenchman Perrot heard a story from an Attic peasant in which Aphrodite appears.[18]   A beautiful queen had a castle at Daphni near Athens and also owned Acro-Corinth, the two places being connected by a subterranean passage.   Two kings were her suitors, one of whom she favored.   Fearful of arousing the other's jealousy, she asked both to help in building a palace on the Acro-Corinth.   To the unfavored suitor she gave what she thought was the harder task, the building of the fortification walls around the top, to the other she gave the construction of a well, and promised to wed the one who finished first.   But the well was to prove the more difficult task.   When the walls lacked only the keystone of the gateway arch, the queen persuaded the unfavored lover, now within reach of the prize, to stop, and kept him occupied until the well was finished.   Pausanias mentions a temple of Aphrodite near the present Daphni, the ruins of which have been excavated, and many writers speak of her temple on Acro-Corinth.   Euripides speaks of Acro-Corinth as the "sacred hill and habitation of Aphrodite."   Her cult statue appears on imperial coins of the neighboring city of Corinth, which was an important center of her worship.

Apollo, the embodiment of radiant youth, the archer-god, prophet and revealer of the future, is still known on the island of Syra as "the god of Delos." Thus Bent says it is "a common belief among the peasants that the ghosts of the ancient Greeks come once a year from all parts of Greece to worship at Delos . . . and even to-day they will reverently speak of the god on Delos."

The marriage functions of Hera, queen of heaven and guardian of women, have been largely transferred to St. Catharine, who is not only the patroness of love, but of marriage. On the eve of the saint's day, November 26, young women are wont to bake a cake with salt as one of its chief ingredients. This they eat and then drink great quantities of water. In the troubled sleep which follows they believe they will see their future husbands.

A curious variant of the old legend of Athena's birth from the head of Zeus is found in a story recounted by Schmidt. A maiden, fully armed, carrying lance and helmet, is born of the swollen leg of an unmarried king. The story appears to have grown out of genuine tradition and is not the result of scholastic influence. It has doubtless also been influenced by the story of the birth of Dionysus from the thigh of Zeus.

Pan, the Arcadian goat-legged god of shepherds, appears to live on as the protector of wild goats and hares, especially on Mount Parnassus. The ears of such beasts are sometimes slit or partly closed, and such mutilations are believed to be signs of ownership on the part of this deity. Longus mentions the sacred flock of Pan, and Pausanias speaks of the cave of Pan near Marathon where the stalactite rocks resemble his herd of goats. To-day, an evil spirit known as *Harm,* in the form of a large he-goat with a long beard, leaps upon the goats and kills them, which belief seems to be a reminiscence of a more malignant aspect of the god Pan. The shepherds have seen him and heard the goats cry with pain. At times the spirit mimics the call or the flute of the shepherds and so draws the herd after him. No one dares to shoot him, lest his gun explode. In the Peloponnesus there is a similar dæmon known as *smigdraki,* but here he does not have the characteristics of Pan, but those of a snake, and he injures not only sheep and goats, but also bees. Holy water protects both shepherd and flocks from his attacks. Schmidt recounts a tale about a goatherd who is presented by Panos with a kid which has a golden fleece. This he sacrifices to God, an angel promising him that he will in return receive any gift he names. He chooses a magic flute, which protects him from all harm, for it can make all who hear it dance. Imprisoned by the king, the goatherd plays and even the houses and rocks begin to dance and every one is crushed. This magic flute seems to be a reminiscence of the pipes of the old god Pan.

We now come to the much debated question of how far the Christian saints have replaced the old gods. It may be said at the outset that the notion that the Church openly substituted saints for the dispossessed gods of similar names and attributes, as voiced by Gruppe and other scholars, has been greatly exaggerated. Similarity in name and function did, in many cases, help the blending of saint and god, but it should certainly not be regarded as a general and acknowledged policy of the Church. Sometimes the Church would recognize the special sphere of a saint and make it of general application, but more frequently the blend must have been merely the result of local conditions, the allocation of the saint's function be-

ing due to local legend. Miss Mary Hamilton
has made this clear in her investigation of the
five chief examples of saints whose names are
supposed to point to pagan gods,—Dionysius,
Demetrius, Artemidus, Eleutherius, and Elias.
We shall briefly consider these in the light of
the evidence.

Gruppe has cited Dionysius as an excellent
example of the theory that saints were directly
evolved out of gods. The connection primarily
rests upon a story still current on Naxos, the
legendary home of Dionysus and one of the
chief centers of his cult. Bent found that St.
Dionysius was there worshipped and popularly
connected with the origin of the vine as his al-
leged namesake was. The saint once jour-
neyed from Olympus to Naxos, and in the heat
of a certain day sat down to rest. Close by he
found and dug up a pretty plant, which he
placed in the bone of a bird to protect it from
the sun. As the plant sprouted he encased it
in the leg-bone of a lion, and finally in that of
an ass. When he planted it on Naxos he could
not separate it from the enveloping bones. As
it grew and bore grapes he discovered the first
wine. The resulting intoxication had three
stages corresponding with the three bones: in

the first a man would sing like a bird, in the second feel as strong as a lion, and, lastly, as foolish as an ass. Lawson argues from this story the thin disguise of the pagan god under the Christian saint, whose name is "changed by an iota, but his character not a jot." But Miss Hamilton has not found the connection so obvious. In the *Synaxarium Ecclesiæ Constantinopolitanæ* there appear three saints of the name, one the Areopagite, another the patron of Zante, and the third a twelfth century monk of Meteora in Thessaly. The journey from Olympus seems to connect the story with the last mentioned one, since the monk had a monastery on Olympus, and is believed to have rid the mountain of bears. But he had no Bacchic attributes, and so the connection with Dionysus in popular tradition must be later in date and purely local. The Naxians would long remember the wine-god, and, on hearing of a similarly named saint, would attach to him the wine-god's attributes, and the local tradition thus gradually became general.

A similar case is that of St. Demetrius, popularly regarded as the patron of farmers and shepherds and the protector of agriculture, and consequently, despite the change in sex, the

descendant of Demeter. There are several
churches in his honor, one of which is at
Eleusis. But the saint cannot have been given
by the Church to its converts as the representa-
tive of Demeter. A martyr, named Demetrius,
was killed in Rome on October 26 of a certain
year, but had no connection with agriculture.
The saint's festival falls in October, but at a
date too late for the harvest, even if the festival in his honor is celebrated by the agricultural classes. At Salonica, where Demetrius
is patron saint, he has no connection with agriculture. Consequently this character must
have originated through association with the
old goddess Demeter, and the blending was
facilitated by the similarity of names. There
may have been some local tradition about
Demeter having been transformed into the
saint. But at Eleusis, the center of Demeter's
rites, we learn of a St. Demetra, uncanonized
and known nowhere else. Down to the beginning of the nineteenth century the peasants
there worshipped a mutilated ancient statue of
the goddess, crowning it with garlands in the
hope of good harvests. In 1801 two English
travelers, despite active opposition by the
peasants, succeeded in removing the statue to

England, where it now rests in the Fitzwilliam Museum in Cambridge.

Another example is St. Artemidus, who is commonly believed to have been evolved out of Artemis. On the island of Ceos (Zea) Bent found St. Artemidus reverenced as the patron of weakly children, and there a church is dedicated to him near the town whither a mother will carry her child which is afflicted by any mysterious sickness, "struck by the Nereids," as they say. She strips and reclothes the child, leaving the old clothes behind. If the child grows strong, the mother thanks the saint, thus unconsciously perpetuating, as Bent believed, the memory of the Ephesian Artemis, who protected children, animals, and vegetation. However, the custom he mentions is by no means confined to Ceos, but is found elsewhere, and is sometimes connected with other saints, *e. g.*, with St. Elias at Chalcis. Consequently we do not have sufficient evidence to assume that the attributes of Artemis have been transferred to the saint.

St. Eleutherius, who is now invoked by women in childbirth, bears a name assumed to be connected with Ilithyia, the goddess of childbirth, one of whose epithets Eleutho, "the freer," is quite similar. Crete is given by some ancient writers as the birthplace of Ilithyia, and in Crete Eleutherius is the patron saint of mothers, especially at childbirth. There and also at the Small Metropolis or Old Cathedral of Athens, dedicated to the Virgin and to St. Eleutherius, women celebrate the latter's festival with offerings. However, this function of the saint is local and there is no evidence of it elsewhere in Greece nor in the biography of the saint. The same function is attributed to St. Stylianus at Arachova and in other places to the Panaghia. So popular legend and local practice explain the similar function caused by similarity in name. A sanctuary of Ilithyia stood near the site of the Small Metropolis and nearby there has been found a statue-base dedicated to her. Thus in localities where she was worshipped as patroness of mothers in childbirth, as in Athens and in Crete, the saint who locally replaced her received a similar function because of the similarity in name; to that extent, then, the saint is an outgrowth of the old divinity, although he did not generally replace the goddess.

The case of St. Elias is more difficult to determine. He has his chapels on many hill-tops of Greece, and popularly is believed to have power over sunlight, rain, and thunder, the latter being ascribed to the rolling of his chariot wheels. The sites of his chapels are where the sunlight lasts longest and the rain first appears. His festival falls during the heat of summer, July 20, and in periods of drought people flock to his shrines to pray for rain. Rain-charms are sometimes employed and also sun-charms or fire-festivals, as on Mount Taÿgetus where a bonfire is lit. All this appears to connect him with Helius, the old Sun-god, and advocates of the theory point to the correspondence in the present pronunciation of Elias and Helius, identical in the genitive. Of course defenders of this theory admit that in the cult of the old nature god there is also embodied the popular concept of Elijah, the greatest of the Hebrew prophets, who brought rain to famine-stricken Palestine and called down fire to consume his own sacrifice, and who finally was translated in a whirlwind to heaven from Mt. Carmel in a fiery chariot drawn by horses of fire. To Greeks accustomed to worship Helius with his fiery chariot, the name of Elias recalled the old god. Sacred icons still picture him in a chariot driven by fiery horses. But other scholars

have denied all connection between Elias and
Helius.   They point out that the cult of Helius
was never as popular in antiquity as that of
Elias is now, and that there is little evidence
to show that Helius was ever worshipped on
mountain-tops.   They think the story of Elijah
is sufficient to have made him the patron of
high places.   But Delehaye's contention that
the Helius cult was almost completely absorbed
in the worship of Apollo is untrue, since, on
the contrary, it grew in later antiquity, especially in connection with the cult of Mithras.
We also know that a peak of Mount Taÿgetus,
known as Taletum, was sacred to Helius, since
Pausanias says that horses were there sacrificed to the god.   Here, there is now a chapel
of Elias, which proves that one place at least
where Helius was formerly worshipped has
been transferred to the saint.   Perhaps the
assimilation was local at first and later the
fame of the nature saint was expanded to in-
clude Helius.   Thus, it seems probable that
St. Elias is remotely connected with Helius, but
that he has been influenced mostly by the
biblical story of Elijah.

Frequently a Greek saint has functions
which seem to have been borrowed directly

from classical legends. There are many such examples recorded in the *Acta Sanctorum*. Thus, St. George of Cappadocia has a military character, and legends about him make him akin to the Greek Perseus, if not to the Egyptian Horus. His icons frequently represent him on horseback slaying a dragon, thus recalling Horus on horseback slaying a crocodile; but this similarity does not prove identity, since most warrior saints are on horseback. At Arachova he frees war-prisoners and protects the sick and lowly. At Argostoli on Cephalonia and on Paros he goes by the name of the "Drunkard," and at his festival on the latter site, which falls on November 3, the date of the saint's death, there is much drinking, for then the new wine is drawn. This seems to show a connection with Dionysus. Near Calamata the saint has a chapel, and the story goes that formerly during his annual celebration on April 23 a local genius used to appear out of the ground and devour a devotee, until St. George confined the monster by placing a large stone over the hole on which was the imprint of his horse's hoof. Hence the saint received his name *Petalotes*, the "shoeing-smith."

St. Hippolytus was fabled to have been torn

by horses, just as Hippolytus was in Athenian legend. St. Nicetas recalls Bellerophon and Pegasus, since he rides through the air on a white-winged horse during his festival on April 3. In fact, he has a chapel on Helicon near the old fountain of Hippocrene. Cosmas and Damian, the chief healing saints of the Greeks, known as the "feeless," are akin to Asclepius and to the Dioscuri. They were two Arab doctors who were converted to Christianity and travelled over the Greek world curing the sick, finally suffering martyrdom in Cilicia in 287. They had many churches, those at Constantinople and Rome being especially celebrated. One of the six at Constantinople was famous as early as 516, when Justinian restored it in gratitude for being cured there. In popular imagination these saints are regarded as kindly genii helpful to man, just as Castor and Polydeuces were in antiquity. In fact the Dioscuri had a temple in Constantinople where incubation was practiced.[19] Thus these kindly gods were blended with the benevolent saints.

St. Nicolas has largely replaced the functions of Poseidon. Sailors pray to him before making a voyage or when in danger, and so he is known as "the Sailor." All Greek boats

have his icons in the stern or on the mast.
Models of boats and gear are his usual votive
offerings. Nicolas was a bishop of Myra and
got his power over the sea from a miracle oc-
curring in his life-time, when he once calmed
the storm which threatened a ship upon which
he was journeying. Before his time sailors
had venerated a St. Phocas, who was originally
a sailor. At first Nicolas was connected more
with Artemis than with Poseidon; as bishop
of Myra and later of Ætolia he fought against
her cult. At the village of Cephalóvryso in
Ætolia, near the ruins of the ancient Thermon,
there is a ruined chapel of St. Nicolas standing
on the site of a temple of Artemis, as we learn
from an inscription. Similarly, near the old
harbor of Aulis, a ruined Byzantine chapel in
his honor is supposed by Ulrichs to have replaced the old Artemisium, where Agamemnon
was on the point of sacrificing his daughter
Iphigenia.

St. Pelagia of Antioch, whose festival falls
on October 8, has been connected by Usener [20]
with Aphrodite. He believes that the Church
continued under modified form to pay homage
to the old goddess of carnal pleasure and animal fecundity. But Delehaye is against the

[83]

contention and points out that there were three saints of the name. One of these was the subject of a famous legend. She was a celebrated dancing girl of Antioch; at the height of her fame she suddenly became converted by Bishop Nonnus whom she heard preaching in front of a church which she and her roistering companions were passing. Being baptized, she retired in the guise of a man to a cave on the Mount of Olives at Jerusalem, where, under the name of Pelagius, she lived three years until her death.

Certain other saints appear to have received their names from those of gods or ancient festivals. Thus St. Rousalia is named from the festival which was celebrated at Athens until recently. St. Donatus is connected with Ædoneus (Hades), his chief churches being situated in the valley of the Acheron in Epirus. St. Venere, invoked by Albanian girls as patroness of marriage, is connected with the Roman Venus. St. Mercurius shows certain attributes of Hermes. At first he was a messenger of Christ, said to have been sent to slay the emperor Julian. Now he is merely the healer of ear diseases on Samos. Hermes' function as the guide of souls below has fallen not

to Mercurius but to St. Michæl. Near Tænarum in Maina at the mouth of a cave which is
supposed to be an entrance to Hades, he stands
on guard, with a sword, instead of the cadu-
ceus, in his hand.

Despite the fact, then, that the Christian
saints have in general replaced the pagan gods,
we have shown that it is very difficult to prove,
in any particular case, that the saints were directly evolved out of gods or that the Church
has deliberately substituted a saint for a god
because of similarity in name or function. The
process of assimilation was somewhat different,
growing gradually out of a folk-consciousness.

III.   THE GREEK CHURCH
FESTIVALS

THE MODERN Greeks more than any other Christian people have retained pagan festivals, for many of the Eastern Church celebrations are merely the survivals of ancient ones, and are often held at churches or monasteries whose saints have taken the place of the old gods. The very name for festival, *panegyri,* is merely the diminutive form of the old name *panegyris,*— that is, an "assembly of the whole people" of the old City-State for the purpose of worship. Furthermore, modern festivals often show the same mixture of religion and art, athletics and trade, as their prototypes showed in antiquity.

These festivals fall on saints' days, and, in the rural districts, are commonly held at the saint's chapel. Local poets or wandering minstrels, the latter the fast disappearing descendants of the Homeric rhapsodes, improvise songs to the accompaniment of a simple

lyre, singing, it may be, the heroic deeds of
the Clephts, the famous Greek outlaws against
the Turks. The attendant fairs attract
crowds of country-folk who come to trade.
Dances are still one of the main features, taking place either on some paved threshing-floor
near the chapel or on the green within or near
its precincts. The most popular dance, the
syrtós, goes back to antiquity. Some of these
festivals, like those at Olympia and Delphi in
antiquity, have become national in scope and
some take place on the very spots where ancient ones were held, as that in honor of the
Panaghia on Ithome where once a festival was
held in honor of Zeus. This festival lasts for
several days and huts are erected near the
church to house the crowds. More often the
women sleep within the church, as at the
church of the Panaghia of Agiasó on Lesbos.
Meals are taken in picnic style, the crowds being seated on stone benches around stone
tables, as at the church of the Panaghia Pala-
tiani on Cos. This method of dining recalls
the "large banquet rooms" at Poseidon's shrine
on Tenos mentioned by Strabo, erected there
to take care of the multitudes who repaired
thither from the neighborhood. Many of the

present festivals have their origin in ancient Roman ones, since these spread over Greek lands, but others just as certainly are descended from Greek prototypes. We shall briefly consider examples of each.

The most important festival of the Greek Church is the twelve-day holiday extending from Christmas to Epiphany. It coincides with several pagan festivals, notably with the Roman *Saturnalia*. Under the Roman Empire the festival of the winter solstice opened in Rome with the *Saturnalia*, a festival which had flourished for many centuries before in the Republic and which later, with the spread of Roman rule, was taken over by the Greeks. Saturn, who, according to tradition, introduced agriculture into Italy, was an early harvest god whose rustic celebration, originally falling on December 19, gradually expanded into the *Saturnalia*. The latter in Augustus' time were held, in connection with the *Opalia*, in honor of Ops, from December 17 to 20, but later popularly from December 17 to 23. Later Greek and Roman writers, such as the antiquary Macrobius, wrongly identified the festival with the old Greek *Cronia*, merely replacing Saturn with Cronus. Macrobius, quoting

Philochorus, states that after sacrifice had been made to Saturn and Ops, *"et frugibus et fructibus iam coactis,"* heads of families were accustomed to sit at table with their slaves. From this phrase, "after grain and fruits have been collected," August Mommsen [21] has argued for two Greek festivals known as the *Cronia,* one of which was celebrated—as we learn from a scholium on Demosthenes—after the harvest, on the 12th of Hecatombæon, *i. e.,* at the end of July or beginning of August, while the other, after the first harvest, he has assigned to the beginning of winter. But there is really no evidence for the existence of this later *Cronia* at all; Macrobius' statement can be referred to the festival falling in the latter part of the summer when the corn and early fruits have been gathered. But even the known summer *Cronia* were never important, as is shown by the fact that few writers mention this festival. Moreover, the only real resemblance between the *Cronia* and the *Saturnalia* was the freedom allowed slaves; but even that was characteristic of several other Greek festivals, such as one held in Crete in honor of Hermes. Since the *Cronia* had ceased by the time of Lucian and Plutarch, when we meet the name in these later writers we are not to understand the Greek festival, but the Roman *Saturnalia*, translated by the old Greek word. Thus it is clear that the Christmas season is to be connected with the Roman, and not with the Greek festival.

The *Saturnalia* were regarded as commemorative of the happy days under Saturn, when equality reigned and violence and oppression were unknown. During the celebration schools and courts were closed, no wars were declared nor battles fought, and no malefactors were tried or punished. In short it was a time for relaxation and unrestrained merriment, when only the most necessary work was performed and only that which conduced to pleasure and amusement. Equality was observed in all classes; slaves sat at their masters' tables, where they were served by them or their guests and had freedom of speech. Gifts were exchanged, and drinking, gambling, singing, and practical jokes were the order of the day. Many of these characteristics reappear in the Greek Christmas of to-day.

At Rome the *Saturnalia* were followed by the most popular of festivals, the *Kalendœ*, falling on New Year's Day, and the *Vota*, falling on January 3. By the third century A. D. these were celebrated on an extensive scale with gaiety and the exchange of gifts. Early Church canons mention them, especially one passed at a synod held in 652, which tried to abolish them along with several others by prohibiting dances and rites after the ancient manner, *i. e.*, masquerading, drunken revels, calling on Dionysus, etc., all of which prove the survival of Dionysiac rites at such celebrations. These festivals resemble the gaiety of the modern New Year's in many ways. Nowadays, Greek villages are decorated, banquets are held, gambling is indulged in, singing and masquerading are popular, and gifts are exchanged.

The Christmas part of these festivities was for a long time relatively unimportant in the Eastern Church. Only recently, under Western influence, has Christmas increased in popularity. We hear of Christmas in the Western Church as being celebrated on December 25 for the first time in 354 A. D., and somewhat later in the Eastern Church. Thus John Chrysostom in his Christmas sermon of 388 says it was introduced at Antioch from the West less than ten years before. Before that date the birth of Christ had been celebrated on Epiphany Day, January 6. In ancient Greece there had been a Sun-festival known as the *Helia* celebrated on December 25. The Sun-god later became identified with the Persian Mithras, whose cult was the greatest rival of Christianity, since the rites of Mithraism were similar and likewise taught immortality. Aurelian, in the third century, blended Helius with Mithraic beliefs, having built a temple in the *Campus Martius* at Rome which was dedicated on the god's supposed birthday, December 25. But the cult waned before the growing power of Christianity. Augustine warned the Christians not to worship the day of the Sun, but that of Him who made the Sun. The Sun-festival, however, was taken over by the Church, and historically Christmas, New Year's, and the days between are connected not only with the *Saturnalia* and *Kalendæ,* but also with the *Helia,* and therefore show an origin largely pagan.

New Year's is now dedicated to St. Basil. On the evening before, bands of boys go from house to house singing a song of the birth of Christ, which ends with good wishes for the coming year and requests for gifts from the house occupants. In Athens they carry a model of a ship, which may refer to the first verse of the song, "St. Basil is come from Cæsarea," or may go back to the worship of Theseus which was instituted in the sixth century B. C. at Athens by Pisistratus, when the ship of the Cretan voyage played a rôle in the Panathenaic festival. In Athens New Year's is a very gay occasion. On the day before, Hermes Street is crowded with people carrying all sorts of noise-producing devices and throwing quantities of confetti. Cakes with coins inside, like the old English Twelfth-night cakes, are prepared in every house, cut up at midnight, and distributed. The person drawing the portion containing the coin is regarded as lucky. At ten o'clock the next day crowds of townspeople follow the royal family—escorted by the *Evzoni* or royal guards, foreign diplomats, ministers and deputies of the State—to the Metropolis Church to worship. Later the King and his family return to the palace, where, at noon, a levee is held which the military and naval officers attend.

Epiphany, the commemoration of Christ's baptism, is now called the "Feast of Lights." In many parts of Greece there takes place a peculiar ceremony known as "Blessing of the Waters," which recalls the old Greek rain-charms. On the island of Imbrus there is a regular rain-charm ceremony, when townsmen and visitors may get a wetting. A girl, dressed in leaves and flowers, leads a procession of other girls through the village. Water is poured over her from every house and the whole band of girls sings. On the Turkish island of Castellorizo east of Rhodes a rain-charm is supervised by the Church. One of the most picturesque ceremonies takes place at the Church of the Transfiguration in the harbor of Syra and has been described by Lucy Garnett. By eight o'clock on the morning of Epiphany day the church is crowded; on a platform in the nave there is placed, adorned with branches and leaves, a pictorial representation of Christ's baptism along with a silver bowl over which a dove is suspended. After the liturgy is over the priests ascend the dais and read the Epistle and Gospel of the day. The bishop blesses the bowl of water and every one present endeavors to secure some of the holy water. Later a procession is led by a band of musicians, and the priests, preceded by acolytes with silver lamps and censers, carry a large cross to the water front, the way thither being lined by soldiers with their bayonets fixed. The cross is then cast into the sea, and whoever dives and recovers it may keep it for the day and collect contributions in recognition of the feat. The purpose of this and similar ceremonies at Phalerum, Athens, and elsewhere is merely to ensure fine weather. Something similar occurred anciently in times of drought in the cult of Zeus Lycæus in Arcadia. Pausanias tells how the priest used to go to the spring Hagno on top of Mount Lycæus to pray and sacrifice and let down into the water an oak-branch, whose stirring would cause a mist to arise, the precursor of rain-clouds. In the modern ceremony the Christian cross has taken the place of the ancient oak-branch, sacred to Zeus.

We next turn to the Easter festivities of the Eastern Church. They are ushered in by the long period of abstinence known as the "Great Fast" or Lent, which, since the seventh century, has lasted for forty days. The two Sundays preceding Lent are known as "Meat Sunday" and "Cheese Sunday" respectively, and the week between them, called "Cheese-eating week," corresponds with the Carnival of the

Western Church. The celebration of the Carnival varies in different parts of Greece. Only
in Athens and a few other large towns is it
celebrated in the Roman Church fashion with
parades, confetti battles, and masked balls.
One must go to the country to see the classical
survivals, especially the Bacchic reminiscences.
R. M. Dawkins [22] has discovered such survivals in certain Thracian villages, especially at
Viza, the site of the ancient Bizya, capital of
the tribe of the Asti. Here on "Cheese Mon-
day" before the village church a drama is en-
acted in which there are many Bacchic reminiscences—the goat-skin head disguises of the
two chief actors, the marriage and mimetic
slaying of one of them, the mourning over his
body by his wife, and his resurrection. Then
the mummers yoke themselves to a plough and
pray for good harvests as they draw it along.
Even a cradle, called the *likni,* contains the
effigy of a babe born out of wedlock and recalls
the fan-shaped basket (λίκνον) in which Dionysus, the natural son of Semele, was fabled to
have been carried. Similar Bacchic survivals
have been found also at a festival celebrated in
honor of Constantine, the patron saint of Costi,
a village of Thrace on the Black Sea coast.

Here the priests known as *Anastenaria* play the chief rôle with dancing images of the saint. The dance gradually grows frenzied, and finally the priests flee, disappearing over the fields "like birds." Only those who thus become possessed can join the ascetic brotherhood of priests. Such frenzied dances and Mænad flights, despite certain Christian rites and the use of images, vividly recall the worship of the old Wine-god.

Lent is celebrated strictly in respect to diet and amusements. It ends Holy Week, whose solemnities culminate in Easter Sunday. Good, or rather "Great," Friday, as it is called by the Orthodox, that is, Crucifixion Day, is the chief day of the week when every one goes to church to reverence the silk-cloth—*epitaphios*—on which the entombment is pictured. Then ceremonies of penance are performed and mourning is shown by burial processions, the tolling of bells, the singing of dirges, the kissing the bier, etc. At midnight of Saturday the Resurrection, the central doctrine of Orthodox Christianity, is celebrated, and again repeated on Easter noon, when the Church has returned to gaiety, as is shown by feasting, the firing of guns, and general relaxation. The Easter ceremonies last over the following Tuesday, when the townsfolk go into the country, where the boys and girls dance, and the youths shoot at a mark or indulge in athletic sports.

Many scholars have traced the celebration of the Carnival back to the Roman *Saturnalia*. Thus Frazer [23] is led to believe that it may be merely "the continuation, under a thin disguise, of a period of temperance which was usually observed, from superstitious motives, by Italian farmers long before the Christian era." He believes that the old Roman festival, although throughout the historical period it was always celebrated in December, at a remote date may have been celebrated in February or March, approximately the date of the modern Carnival. Of this, however, he admits there is no direct evidence. But the Eastern Lent might better be compared with the fast which preceded the celebration of the Eleusinian mysteries, commemorating Demeter's period of abstinence from food during her search for her ravished daughter Persephone. The *Lesser Eleusinia*—originally the Attic mysteries of Agræ, held on the banks of the Ilissus—symbolized the resurrection of nature, and their celebration took place during the middle of the month of

Anthesterion (the end of February and beginning of March), that is, about the date of
Easter, when Coré (Persephone) was supposed
to return in the young corn.

The Easter rites of crucifixion and resurrection also have their counterparts in the ancient
worship of Attis and Cybele. This cult was
popular at Rome, where the festival lasted
several days at about the time of the spring
equinox. An effigy of the dead Attis was tied
to a pine-tree which was felled in the woods,
and, adorned with violets, the sacred flowers
of the god, was brought to the temple of Cybele.
March 24 was a "day of blood" when the devotees cut themselves with knives, as the
Persian dervishes do now. The effigy was
burnt and the fast kept up till night, when the
mourning was turned into joy, and the carnival
of the *Hilaria* began the following day. On
the 27th a procession took place to the sacred
brook Almo in the Campagna where the image
of Cybele was bathed by the priests, that is,
a spring rain-charm was performed connected
with Attis as a god of vegetation, whose return
signified the revival of the crops. So the rites
now celebrated at Easter are doubtless connected in some ways with several pagan festi-

vals. Identification with any of these is, however, scarcely possible, as the evidence is slen-
der. We know that in antiquity abstinence
from food and from the gratification of the
appetites was practiced by many peoples at
seed-time for the purpose of promoting the
growth of the crops, that is, as a sort of charm.
Easter now is a "paschal" feast which goes
back to the Hebrew Passover *("Pesach")*.
The early Christians refused to celebrate the
Jewish feast and only recognized the Resurrection. The two are separated in early Church
calendars, the Resurrection being the movable
Jewish Passover, being assigned at first to
March 27, and the Crucifixion to March 25.
But there is no historical reason for the death
of Jesus being placed at that date. The date
may well have come in some way from the
Roman cult of Attis, which has to some extent
supplanted the Christian Easter.

Another important Greek festival is the
"Assumption of the Virgin," poetically called
by the Greeks the "Falling Asleep of the
Virgin," which is universally celebrated in
the Eastern Church on August 15. We shall
briefly describe its celebration at the monastery
of Vourkano on Mount Ithome in Messenia.

3 4178

According to a tradition preserved by the monks of Mount Eva a burning tree was seen one night on the opposite ridge. Crossing over they found an icon of the Panaghia hanging to a tree with a lighted candle beside it, and they brought the icon to their monastery. It soon, however, found its way back again, which showed the monks that it was the Virgin's will to change the location of the monastery. This is now at Vourkano, which is situated on the Eastern slope of the mountain just below the saddle between the two peaks of Ithome and Eva. On the top of Ithome was the old precinct of Zeus Ithomatas. The tree-trunk on which the icon was found hanging is now the lintel of the doorway of the monastery, badly hacked by the faithful who believe that the wood can cure fevers. A fast precedes the Assumption, beginning August 6. On the 12th the icon is carried in procession around the country-side, and sheep, goats, and oxen are sacrificed. Three days later it is returned to the monastery. But on the 24th it again goes on its travels, being taken to the town of Nisi near Calamata where the festival is concluded with a fair.

The origin of this festival is to be found in

an ancient harvest celebration. At Arachova on August 6 first-fruits of the wheat crop are offered to the Panaghia, and wheat cannot be eaten until it has been blessed by the priest on that day. On Zante wheat and currants are put in a basket together with a burning candle and taken to church on August 15. The priest blesses it and places a part on the altar and distributes the rest. The cakes known as *Kolyva* —a mixture of wheat and grain, which we shall discuss further on—are brought on August 6 to all churches for blessing, and are then divided and eaten by the congregation. Such cake-offerings can be traced to the sixth century in connection with the Assumption, and seem to be the survival of first-fruit offerings, such as those offered the Syrian goddess of agriculture, and now transferred to Mary.

A festival which shows clear survivals of pagan rites is the one held on March 25, at the Church of Our Lady of Annunciation on the island of Tenos in the Cyclades. This picturesque festival has been described by many visitors, notably by Miss Hamilton. Pilgrims flock hither from mainland Greece, the islands, Asia Minor, Egypt, and even Turkey, thus recalling the ancient pilgrimage to the nearby

island of Delos, which was the chief event of
the old Greek religious year. The fame of
this modern Mecca is only a century old, since
the church is dated traditionally back to the
day on which the Greek Revolution was declared. The usual dream preceded the foundation of the church, when the Virgin appeared
to an islander and directed him to search at a
particular spot for her icon. He was unsuccess-
ful in his search, but later a nun was given the
same directions in three dreams, and the icon
was finally found. It was in a very dilapidated
condition, as it was cut in twain and had been
scorched in the invasion of the Saracens. Still
it has been regarded ever since as a masterpiece
of St. Luke, to whom so many of the venerated
icons of the Greek Church are ascribed. The
chapel and well on whose site the church was
built belonged to an older one of St. John,
burnt in 1200. But many marble fragments
show that in antiquity the site was that of a
temple. It is now the wealthiest church in
Greece, since many millions of drachmæ are
donated to it each year. Much of this money
is converted into precious stones which are set
in the frame around the icon. A paved way
leads up to the church, along which pilgrims

frequently creep on hands and knees, suffering from lameness, which is the chief ill supposed to be cured. The usual neighborhood fair is held in booths where all sorts of articles are sold to the visitors, especially silver crucifixes, and models of parts of the body. Various amusements are also offered. The pilgrims are cared for at night inside or outside the church, in the porticoes of the monastery and else-where, where mattresses are laid for the sick,—each bringing his own bed, cooking utensils, and food.

The icon is enclosed in a gilded box covered over with glass and stands on a small altar. It is twelve by eighteen inches in size and only the head, scarcely recognizable, is visible. The lid is devotedly kissed. On the evening before Annunciation Day the Panaghia is supposed to make her cures. The vigil begins at eight, when church and crypt are filled. The latter is a long, dark room where rows of people stand on either side, leaving free a center aisle up and down which the streams of pilgrims go to the altar and back. Despite the number of visitors—now perhaps 4,000 to 5,000 a year, although formerly there were many more—only a few miracles of healing are recorded. Lawson gives the official number down to the year 1898 as forty-four, which is considerably less than one a year since the founding of the church. Of these, twelve were cases of insanity, eleven of blindness, and ten of paralysis. But various visitors report having seen many who had come with crutches depart without them. Patients often remain a long time, one paralytic sailor being said to have remained four months, until his patience was rewarded with a cure. At dawn of the next day the icon is carried in procession through the village, and a last opportunity is thus given to the expectant pilgrims to receive the Virgin's blessing, as the shadow of the icon falls upon them along the way. Sometimes the icon fares further afield. During the serious illness of King Constantine in 1917, it was carried to Athens by a bishop and placed at the king's head with the hope that thereby a cure might be effected. Those baffled at Tenos do not give up, however, but frequently go to some other church with the hope of being cured by some other icon. Just so in antiquity valetudinarians travelled from shrine to shrine. Thus Aristides, the friend of Marcus Aurelius, spent a large part of his life visiting temples in quest of health. His six *Sermones sacri* form a diary of his thirteen years of illness and ultimate recovery.

This festival on Tenos is one of the best examples of the survival of an ancient religious custom. For passing the night in or near the church in the vicinity of the icon of the Virgin with the hope of being cured of disease recalls the old temple-sleep or incubation.[24] The custom, although not universal, was widespread in antiquity, and centered in the belief that while the patient was asleep the soul was released from the body and became more susceptible to divine influence, since the god could thus better enter into communication with his devotee. Uneducated Greeks and Romans, in common with primitive men elsewhere, believed that disease, both physical and mental, was largely the result not of natural causes, but of the interference of an offended deity or malevolent spirit. Such spirits, therefore, had to be driven out by prayer and sacrifice. At the end of antiquity the practice of incubation became very popular, especially under the Empire, when certain healing shrines gained an international reputation. Asclepius surpassed all other healing gods, and his shrines in Epidaurus and on the island of Cos were especially famous; here purificatory rites and medical methods such as therapeutic diet and exercise, helped by the use of narcotics, incense, and even mechanical contrivances, were believed to effect cures. Besides, the temples of Asclepius were generally located in salubrious spots. Similarly, among the modern Greeks many diseases, especially those of a nervous character, are largely ascribed to the influence of dæmons. When a Greek despairs of the ordinary doctor's help he has recourse to the priest in order that the evil spirit may be exorcised through the favor of the local saint. Then, by fasting, prayer, and especially incubation, as anciently, he confidently hopes for relief. Each saint has appropriated a certain sphere in the cure of such diseases, and prescribes certain ceremonies.

Sculptures have always been excluded from the Greek Church, but sacred icons have been allowed to satisfy the instinct for idolatry. They are of a traditional Byzantine type, the work of monks or priests. They are usually conventional, lifeless, and out of proportion and perspective, even though at times they may show great technical skill. Yet, despite their deficiencies there is always something dignified about the poorest of them. Every cottage has its crude icon of a saint before which a tiny' lamp is always kept burning—a custom which recalls an ancient one mentioned by Lucian. If the lamp goes out, it is a sign of impending evil. The kissing of icons also recalls the ancient custom of kissing statues. Cicero speaks of a bronze Heracles at Agrigentum, whose mouth and chin were worn away by kissing, just as is the toe of St. Peter's statue in the Church of Saint Peter at Rome to-day. During Church festivals the icon is adorned with myrtle and laurel, as statues were frequently garlanded in antiquity. The carrying of the icon in procession also has its counterpart in antiquity. Thus the cult statue of the Eleutherian Dionysus at Athens was carried forth on fixed days each year from the city shrine of the god. And many other examples could be cited.

Various relics with curative powers are also carried in procession. Thus, on the island of Zante, Schmidt records that the body of the patron saint is carried through the streets on the anniversary of his death, and that in the village of Phagiá, in the church of St. Marina, an icon exists to which insane folk are brought

on the birthday of the saint. The priest dips
his finger into the oil in front of the icon, and
places the finger upon the lips of the patient,
while he puts his other hand on the patient's
head, and then invokes the saint to cast out the
dæmon. In the church of St. Luke outside
Thebes there is a Hellenistic sarcophagus,
which is believed to be that of the evangelist.
Women kneel before it and receive the marble
scrapings which the priest peels off with his
knife; these are placed in water which is drunk
by children suffering from fever.

An excellent example of prehistoric pillar-
cult is furnished by the chapel of "St. John of
the Column" in Athens. This is built around
an unfluted Corinthian column which projects
through the roof. As the column was found on
the spot, it doubtless belonged to some old
shrine of the Roman period. The chapel is
sacred to John the Baptist, the patron of fevers.
The story runs that the saint, when about to
die, tied all human diseases to the base of a
column by means of silk threads—fevers with
yellow threads, measles with red, etc. He
then said: "When I die, let any sick come
and tie a silk thread to the column and be
healed."

[109]

Sick people come to the chapel and pray, especially on his festival day August 28. They affix colored threads or bits of rags or even locks of hair to the column with wax in the belief that their disease will be transferred to it. Even silver pieces are placed on it, in order to get oracular responses; if they adhere, a cure is promised. The column is covered with offerings during the hot days of August and September when fever is rife. Similarly, Athenian mothers take their sick children to the chapel of St. Marina at the foot of Observatory Hill, undress them and leave their old clothes behind, in the belief that they are thus transferring the disease. Nearby is a smooth inclined rock, polished by generations of women who have slid down it with the idea that it would cure them of barrenness.

It is still the custom in Greece, as it was in antiquity, to hang up models in wax or silver of the parts of the body cured by the saint—arms, hands, feet, eyes, breasts, etc. Grateful mothers even bring small models of their children, just as they did in ancient times. Thus, we read in the *Palatine Anthology* of wax models of a girl and her brother being dedicated by their parents in fulfillment of a vow.

Sailors dedicate models of ships. Tapers, oil, first-fruits of the harvest, and money are constantly offered. At times the icon of a saint may be covered with bits of money stuck on by wax. Lucian mentions a statue of Pelichus, to whose thigh silver coins were affixed with wax, since it was believed to have the power of curing fevers. Great numbers of votive offerings—*anathemata*—were brought to the shrines of the old healing gods, especially models of parts of the body. In the ruins of the temple of Asclepius at Epidaurus there have been found such models and also marble tablets on which the healed part was represented, carved in relief. Metal ones have been found at the shrine of Amphiaraus at Oropus. Lord Aberdeen in 1803 found many such marble relief models on the rock wall of the Pnyx at Athens. Others have found similar ones on the south side of the Acropolis and elsewhere. Such models in terra cotta have been found in various parts of Greece and Italy.

In this brief sketch of a few of the Greek Church festivals we should not omit two minor domestic festivals which show most direct survivals from antiquity, the singing in

procession of the song of the swallow as the
harbinger of spring, and the *Rousalia,* or
"Feast of Roses."

In Macedonia and the Peloponnesus to-day
bands of boys parade the village streets on the
first of March, carrying a painted wooden swallow on the end of a garlanded pole. At the
same time they sing a song congratulating the
people on the return of spring, and ask for
gifts. The same custom existed among the
old Greeks, and one of the swallow-songs, once
popular on Rhodes, where it was sung in the
month of Boëdromion (September-October),
has been preserved to us in the *Deipnosophists*
of Athenæus,[25] beginning

> "*The swallow has come, has come,*
> *Bringing a good season and a joyful time.*
> *Her belly is white, her back is black,*"

and ending

> "*Open, then, open the door to the swallow,*
> *For we are not old men, but boys!*"

One of the present versions, as sung in
Thessaly, is an echo of this. I quote the begin-
.ning of it in the translation of John Addington
Symonds:

"She is here, she is here, the Swallow!
Fair seasons bringing, fair years to follow!
Her belly is white,
Her back, black as night!"

At the end it voices a similar appeal for gifts.

The "Feast of Roses" was celebrated in Athens until recently, around the so-called Theseum on Tuesday of Easter week, which is still a favorite picnic day. The festival did not fall, however, on the day of St. George, the patron of the Theseum. Country-folk came into town carrying musical instruments and sang a song, beginning:

"Good day, Lady mine, and prosperity to you,
my children."

A boy baby was lifted into the air three times with a prayer for its health and that of other children. Later in the day the *Rousalia* were held. In Macedonia, Abbott found the festival celebrated on the twenty-fifth day after Easter and with the definite purpose of warding off scarlatina. Then ring-shaped cakes, called *kolouria*, are made and hung over the house-door. This ceremony, as performed in the village of Melenik, is called *Rousa*—perhaps from the red color of the eruptions in scarlatina, although the word may be a corruption of the Latin *Rosalia*. Pouqueville [26] long ago found the ceremony existing in Epirus, and Miss Hamilton states that the Vlachs still celebrate the festival for six weeks in summer in honor of the dead, when people go to the cemetery and place roses on the graves as we do on Decoration Day. The festival, then, is connected in name with the Roman *Rosalae escae,* "rose food," an annual rose-feast when tombs were adorned, the ceremony of hanging garlands being known as the *Rosalia*. The old name is said to be found still in the Peloponnesus, although there it is not connected with a rose-festival, but with one in honor of the dead, which falls on the Saturday before Whitsunday. Only in Macedonia, where it is connected with children and health, has the festival lost all its earlier association with the dead. The modern festival, therefore, is related in some way to the very ancient Athenian flower-festival known as the *Anthesteria,* which was celebrated in classical times in honor of Dionysus for three days in the month of Anthesterion, corresponding with the first three days of our March. The chief feature of the *Anthesteria* was the procession on the second day which commemorated the entry of Dionysus Eleutherius from outside the city into the small shrine of the god in the Ceramicus. This was followed by his symbolic marriage with Basilinna, the wife of the king archon. The last day's celebration, however, was chiefly in honor of the dead, since it contained a *Thanatousia*. A mixture of corn and honey was placed in a pit and pots of seeds were offered on altars by the priestesses of the Basilinna. On this day the worshippers did not partake of the offerings as they had done on the preceding days, but all offerings were devoted to the dead or to chthonian deities, the main purpose of this oldest part of the celebration being to drive out evil spirts and to ensure good crops.

Enough has been said, then, to show that some of the most important festivals of the Christian Church, such as those of Christmas and Easter, are profoundly influenced by pagan rites which reach back to remote antiquity; and that many features of others celebrated in the Eastern Church, such as the Assumption of the Virgin and the Annunciation, preserve religious customs carried over from ancient prototypes.

IV. DIVINATION AND
SACRIFICE

W E SHALL next briefly consider the practice of divination and sacrifice in modern Greece, both of which show analogies to ancient rites.

Divination, the world-wide practice of rites by which the future is unveiled and the will of supernatural powers is learned, was a common phenomenon of ancient Greek religion. The rites were both natural and artificial. The former depended upon the psychical condition of the diviner, who was believed to be inspired, as the Homeric prophets and the Delphic Pythia; the latter made use of magic and augury, the interpretation of signs and omens, such as the flight of birds or the appearance of the entrails of sacrificed animals.[27]

Of all the means used the oracle was the most important. In Homer's day local oracles were less consulted than individual prophets, because the latter were regarded as directly inspired. But in the historical period the seats of the great oracles were revered as the spots where the gods most clearly disclosed their wills, at Dodona through the rustling of leaves, at Delphi through the disordered utterances of an inspired priestess. While the answers were often vague and cryptic, on the whole these oracles stood for ethical and religious progress, and the interpreting priests were actively interested in the welfare of Greece.

Dreams have always been regarded both by the ignorant man and by the philosopher as revealing the will of supernatural beings. The old Greeks looked upon them as the messengers of Zeus. Pindar and Æschylus mention the well-known idea that during sleep the mind is unfettered and can soar into the realm of spirit and commune with divinity and clearly see the future. Even the scientific Aristotle looked upon dreams as the source of things divine. In later antiquity dreams were scientifically studied. Thus Artemidorus of Ephesus wrote a treatise in five books called *Oneirocritica*, which explains five different classes of dreams. Temple-sleeping, perhaps reaching back as far as Homer, was the chief method of enticing dreams, for then the god was wont to appear and give counsel. The earliest literary evidence of incubation as a part of cult ritual is the *Plutus* of Aristophanes, the scene of which is laid in the temple of Asclepius at Athens or, perhaps, in the Piræus. The gods at whose shrines incubation took place were chthonian, that is, heroes who had died and become invested with earth powers. As we have already remarked, it was most common in shrines of Asclepius; in Hellenistic days it was also common in those of Serapis, an Alexandrine god—who had, as Bouché-Leclercq has aptly said, "a Greek body haunted by an Egyptian soul"—and his accompanying goddess Isis, whose cult flourished in the later ages. It was also practiced at certain oracles, such as those of Amphiaraus at Oropus and Trophonius at Lebadea.

Omens were constantly heeded in antiquity. An unlucky one might delay a battle or a retreat, as the eclipse of the moon destroyed the hopes of the Athenian army at Syracuse. A seer was even more important to an army than the general. The flight of birds, such as the eagle of Zeus, "the surest sign among winged fowl," and the hawk of Apollo, their number, cries, and direction, were common ways of divining according to Homer, but the least important in classical times. The entrails of animals were carefully studied, a science which Greece ultimately owed to Babylonia. Plato regarded the liver as the mirror in which the power of thought was reflected and as the seat of life. It was the Romans, however, who perfected this science, which they borrowed from the Etruscans who had received it from the Orient. The appearance of a snake, as at the sailing of the Greek fleet at Aulis, a chance remark, a sneeze, all were regarded as showing the will of the gods. Casting lots was common in Homer and remained the regular way of voting in democratic Athens throughout the historical period.

It is not too much to say that all these methods of divining reappear in Greece to-day among the common people.

Instead of the inspired prophets of antiquity, nowadays it is insane people who arouse a feeling of awe, since their incoherent utterances are often taken for wise predictions. Such persons are generally regarded as above their fellows and so can live without working. It is now considered lucky to meet one, although in

Theophrastus' day it was unlucky, when one had to spit in his bosom to avert the baleful influence.

To-day the dream is the usual method employed to learn the will of God and his saints. It is the ordinary method in the Church, as we have seen, of revealing the location of sacred icons on spots where churches or monasteries are to be erected. We have already discussed the visitation of Mary to her devotees asleep in her churches. Dream-books, recalling that of Artemidorus, are still popular and may even be found in houses where the Bible is unknown. We have mentioned the custom of girls on the eve of St. Catharine eating salt cakes and drinking wine or water, and then, in their troubled sleep, seeing their future husbands.

There are even survivals of oracles in Greece. The one best known, although it now enjoys only a local fame, is on Amorgus, an isle which enjoyed little ancient fame, as it was a place of exile in the Roman Empire. Here, built over a prophetic stream, is the Church of St. George Balsamites, whose priest is supposed to be able to divine the future. In a side-shrine there is a large square block of marble hollowed out and polished within. It stands on the native rock and is covered with a lid which can be fastened. In the bottom is a hole in which there is a plug. The priest prays to the saint, and then draws some of the water from the receptacle into a cup. According as particles of dirt, insects, hairs, bits of leaves, etc. appear on the surface, the answer is given. Thus, the presence of hair means illness or trouble. At the end of the seventeenth century the oracle was very famed, but the responses were differently given. A Jesuit priest of Santorini, Robert Sauger, has left an account of his visit, published in 1699. Then the cavity filled and emptied itself several times each hour, though he could detect no hole at the bottom. If the consultant found it full when he looked in, the answer was favorable; but if empty, the answer was unfavorable. Sailors from Amorgus and nearby islands are said to consult the oracle yet for the success of voyages, business ventures, etc.

Another method of divination is found at the shrine of the Panaghia at Cremastó on Rhodes. Here the consultant places a coin on the icon. If it sticks, his wish is granted; but in any case the priest gets the coin. It is said that over 6,000 people, including Turks, consult this shrine annually. The moisture which is believed to trickle down the icon at midnight is absorbed in bits of cotton-wool and these are used as amulets. On Zante, near the village of Callipado, Schmidt found an icon of Mary in a rock-grotto, which was revered by the peasants, who placed copper coins against it; if they stuck, the answer was favorable.

The divine power of springs, fountains, and streams was well-known in antiquity. Thus the waters of the Styx were adjured by the immortals, and the sacred springs of Colophon in Ionia, of Hysiæ in Bœotia, and Cassotis at Delphi, were famous. Before consulting the oracle at Delphi pilgrims washed in the fountain of Castalia. Its efficacy is shown by a Pythian response thus translated by Sandys:

"To the pure precincts of Apollo's portal,
  Come, pure in heart, and touch the lustral wave;
One drop sufficeth for the sinless mortal;
All else, e'en Ocean's billows, cannot lave."

The belief that those who drank of it were poetically inspired was a later invention of Roman poets. The belief in the deadly water of certain streams, such as that of the Styx just mentioned, would explain why oaths were sworn by it, since it was a sort of poison ordeal, and it was believed that the water would kill a perjurer. Chemical analysis of the Styx, however, has disclosed no substance in solution, so that the only injury which it could cause is from its coldness, since its glacial water descends from the top of Mount Chelmus, the ancient Aroania. The same notion was at the base of the modern witch ordeal: the suspected person was cast into a pool with a stone attached to her back. If she floated, she was guilty, since the "sacred element" would reject a criminal. Similarly, Ino had a pool near the village of Epidaurus-Limera in Laconia, into which during her festival barley loaves were cast for consultation; if they sank, the water accepted them, and the sign was favorable; but if they floated, the opposite was the case. Zosimus, a historian of the late fifth century, mentions a lake at Aphæa in Syria into which gold, silver, and raiment were cast; these would sink, if accepted, but would float, if rejected. Water from sacred springs is still used in Greece. It comes generally from mineral springs and so has curative qualities, and frequently churches and monasteries are built over such spots. Two such springs are located on the western side of Mount Hymettus, near which are the convents of Cæsariani and Carea, the former dating from the eleventh century. Hither sterile women repaired in antiquity, a practice which is still continued. Ovid mentions one of these springs as a *fons sacer*, and Photius says it was sacred to Aphrodite as healer.

Magic, sorcery, and witchcraft are as common now, especially in Thessaly, as in the time of Theocritus' Simætha. Old crones are still consulted by the love-sick for philtres, incantations, and all sorts of antidotes against spells, and they are always ready to read the stars or to interpret dreams.

No country exists where everyday life is so molded by common superstitions as Greece. We shall mention only a few which have ancient parallels. Hesiod gives a long list of lucky and unlucky days. In Plato's time certain days were presided over by malevolent powers, when certain sorts of work could not be done, and no assembly or court could be held. Thus the last three days of each month were set apart for the chthonian deities, and no enterprise was then begun, for example, in

March, during the Athenian festival of the
Anthesteria, and in June at the *Plynteria,* or
festival of humiliation. The third and thir-
teenth of each month were unlucky, and the
fifth was devoted to the Furies. To-day all
Tuesdays are unlucky, when no hair is cut.
Saturday, the Jewish Sabbath, is especially unlucky in Thessaly and Macedonia. May is
unlucky for marriages, and February is known
as the "lame month," and in some parts of
Greece a child born in that month is expected
to be crippled. In Macedonia all Wednesdays
and Fridays of March are unlucky. All over
Greece on certain days of March and August,
varying somewhat in different places, it is
necessary to abstain from certain sorts of work.
These days, generally the first three or five and
the last three or five of these months, are
known as *Drymiais,* a name which is also applied to vague, though personal spirits supposed to be active at the time. On these days
no trees can be pruned and the peasants do no
washing, fearing lest the clothes will rot, and
they do not bathe lest their bodies will swell.
In August, bathers are armed with a rusty nail
against such spirits. Tylor has regarded the
Drymiais, therefore, as survivals of the Stone

Age, since iron is hostile to such spirits. But
why these particular days are unlucky we cannot say, or what the spirits are from which
they are named. Perhaps these spirits are survivals of the wood nymphs of spring and the
water nymphs of fall. Thus Schmidt has referred them to the old Dryads, whose name
is not dissimilar.

The nails are cut only on certain days in
Greece. Pliny says that they should be cut
only on the nones, and the hair only on the
seventh and ninth of each month. If a mule
foals(!) in the spring, it means calamity; this
idea recalls the story of the foaling of the mule
of Zopyrus, which Herodotus says portended
the fall of Babylon, an unlikely event, though
possible "when mules bore offspring." It is
still unlucky to hear a crow on the housetop,
just as it was in Hesiod's day. A weasel seen
near a Greek house portends evil, although the
opposite is true in Macedonia. Suidas says
that a weasel on the roof portended evil. But
if a snake is found in a house, it is a lucky
sign, for, as we shall see in the next chapter, the
snake is usually regarded as the *genius loci*
now, as it was in antiquity. A dog howling at
night is still the sign of death, as it was in the

days of Theocritus. Crackling logs on the
hearth mean now, as Suidas says they did anciently, that a friend or good news is on the
way. A spluttering candle means misfortune
to-day as it did in Propertius' day.

Involuntary movements of the body still
have their significance. Ringing in the ears
signifies that you are being talked about. If
it be in the left ear it is unfavorable talk, but
if in the right, favorable, although this interpretation is reversed in Macedonia. Lucian
has the same notion. To-day, the twitching of
the eyelid has a meaning similar to that which
it had in antiquity: if it be in the right lid, it
augurs good news or that a friend is expected;
but if in the left, bad news or an enemy. Just
so the lovelorn swain in Theocritus' Idyll feels
his right eye twitch and so hopes to see his
Amaryllis. Sneezing still means prosperity or
the confirmation of what has just been said, on
the theory that an evil spirit has been expelled.
In the *Odyssey*, Telemachus sneezes and con-
firms the words of Penelope. Xenophon accepts the sneeze as a sign of approval from
Zeus. Aristotle, Pliny, Petronius, and many
other writers mention this sign. The superstition continued through the Middle Ages and

is world-wide to-day. The German *"Gesund-heit"* and the English "God bless you" recall the old Greek exclamation "Zeus save you."

The ancient belief in reading the future from the flight of birds has survived. Almost the same birds are believed now, as in antiquity, to reveal the future by their cries, number, direction, etc.,—the eagle, vulture, hawk, crow, and others. One cry may signify prosperity, and three adversity, although in antiquity three meant prosperity. The eagle's scream means conflict, the raven's croak death, the woodpecker's cry intrigue, and the cuckoo's an epidemic. Birds flying on the right still portend success.

Divining by the bones and entrails of animals is nowadays wide-spread from Britain to China and is also common among the American Indians. The use of the shoulder-blade of a lamb or kid is a relic of the ancient haruspication which has survived in Greece and in many other countries. In Britain the art is still known as "reading the speal-bone," where "speal" is a corruption of the French *espaule*. In the seventeenth and eighteenth centuries the outlawed Clephts in Greece still used the shoulder-blade to divine the future, and nowa-

days Greek peasants use it to tell the success
of their crops, the advisability of marriage, and
many other ventures. The bone is cleansed
and held to the light, and its color, veins, spots,
are all full of meaning.

The casting of lots is as old as Homer.
Chance words overheard by the diviner or anyone else are as efficacious now as in antiquity.
A ceremony called *Cledona* takes place on St.
John's day, June 24.[28] A boy is sent the evening before to fetch "speechless" water from
a spring, so-called because he is not to speak to
anyone while bringing it. On his return a
company of girls, who have banded together
to learn the future, drop into the jar, each for
herself, a coin, a ring, a button, or some other
common object, and the jar is left covered for
the night for the Nereids to cast their spell
over it. In the morning each girl sings an
amatory distich, while the person holding the
jar draws out a trinket, and the object so
drawn fits one of the verses sung and will refer
to the girl to whom it belongs. Or she may
stand at the door and listen to the passers-by,
and thus, by a chance name or remark, learn
about her future husband. Again she may
take a salt cake, divide it into three parts and

tie ribbands, red, black, and blue, to the parts, and lay them under her pillow. In the morning she draws a ribband by chance; if a red one, her husband will be a bachelor, if a black one, a widower, and if a blue one, a stranger.

In our opening chapter we mentioned the spirit of bargaining characteristic of ancient sacrifice and prayer. It had been carried to such extremes that it aroused the biting sarcasm of Lucian, who said a poor man propitiated a god by kissing his own hand, while a farmer donated an ox, a shepherd a lamb, a goatherd a goat, and others incense or a cake. "So nothing, it seems, that they (*i. e.*, the gods) do, is done without compensation. They sell men their blessings, and one can buy from them health, it may be, for a calf, wealth for oxen, a royal throne for a hundred." [29] This spirit of bargaining is still prevalent in the Eastern Church, as the great number of votive offerings at Tenos and elsewhere shows. Gifts have generally replaced the old sacrificial animals,— candles and objects of value being presented at churches either for favors already received or for those hoped for. We might mention gold and silver objects, richly bound Bibles, eastern embroideries, models of parts of the body healed, models of houses, ploughs, boats, etc., as thank offerings of to-day. Of the second type to win favors, we might adduce the simple cakes which are set out by women in caves or at home for the Fates or the Nereids, or pork for the Callicantzari. Cake-offerings of the present day certainly go back to antiquity. Two kinds, *kolyva* and *kolloura,* are especially used to appease malevolent spirits, and merit a word of explanation.

We have already spoken briefly of the cakes which still go by their ancient name *kolyva,* and which were used in antiquity for certain festivals. Schmidt found on the Ionian islands reminiscences of these cakes. They are chiefly composed of wheat, but contain many other ingredients, such as raisins, almonds, peas, pomegranate and anise seed, and nuts. They are offered at sowing, at harvest, and at vintage, that is, as a propitiatory and as a thank offering. Such a cake is taken to the church, where a portion of it is crumbled over the altar and the rest is eaten, while, at the same time, every-one present expresses a wish. Thus on Zante the peasants bring such a cake, there called *"sperna"* or vesper offerings, to the church in a basket at the celebration of the

"Holy Transfiguration of Christ" on August
6, and at the "Assumption of the Virgin" on
August 15. It is placed in the center of the
church on a stand with a burning candle
nearby. During mass the priest blesses it and
strews the chancel with a portion of it broken
into crumbs, and distributes the rest among
the people, who eat it and makes a wish. This
ceremony, as we have remarked in the preceding chapter, recalls the "first-fruit" offerings at
certain old Athenian festivals.

Schmidt also recounts a domestic ceremony
on the Ionian islands which takes place on
Christmas day. A large ring-shaped cake, still
known by its ancient name *kolloura*, is made
of wheat, raisins, and almonds. A coin is
baked in it, which belongs to the one who
draws the portion of the cake which contains
it, and hence he is regarded as lucky. Before
the cake is divided and eaten, the father of the
family fills a glass vessel with equal parts of
wine and olive oil, and then, accompanied by
wife and children, he carries the cake to the
hearth, where he pours the liquid three times
through its center into the fire in the form of
the cross, while the family at the same time

[132]

sings a song beginning with the words: "Thy birth, O Christ, the God." Finally the cake is placed upon the table and divided, and everyone makes a wish as he eats his share. Such a hearth ceremony goes back to the old domestic custom of making offerings to Hestia. As the Greek Hestia, whose symbol was the hearth-fire, the religious center of the family, was never so important as her Roman counterpart Vesta, we conclude that the present· ceremony is largely due to Roman influence.

Schmidt also tells of a ceremony which takes place in Arachova on the evening before the festival of the "Presentation of the Virgin" on November 21. A porridge, called *panspermiá*, made of wheat, beans, and lentils, is eaten by the family for the purpose of asking the Virgin for a favorable harvest the following year. This ceremony also appears to be a survival of the offerings of the first-fruits, which were originally made to Demeter or to some agrarian goddess, and which now have been transferred to the Virgin.

Thus we see that many of the rites observed by the Eastern Church and its votaries are in their origin pagan rather than Christian. An-

[133]

cient methods of divination still survive, similar
objects of sacrifice and offering are surren-
dered in the ancient spirit, though incorporated
in the body of the new religion.

V. DÆMONOLOGY: NEREIDS, GENII, GIANTS, AND CALLI-CANTZARI

A LONG with the survivals already discussed as having come into Eastern Christianity from Greek sources, we also find an astonishing body of superstitions about various supernatural powers. Most of these have their origin, of course, in prehistoric animism, the substratum of Greek as of all early religions. Curiously, these beliefs never disappeared from Greek religion even after it had developed into its highest forms and many of them, slightly changed, live on among the Greeks of to-day.

These various supernatural powers surviving from paganism are now known generally as *dæmons,* although other names are also given to them. Thus, a common appellation of these spirits is *ta 'xotiká,* "the outside ones," *i e.,* the non-Christian powers, a term evidently coined by the early Christians. A more literary form of the same idea is found in the New

Testament, *hoi exothen* or *hoi exo*, which refers either to non-Christian powers or to non-Christians. A similar idea is expressed by the term *ta paganá*, "the pagan powers," a term not used, however, on the Ægean islands nor in the Peloponnesus. Other common, but easily understood, names are *ta 'xaphniká*, "the swift comers," *ta angelicá*, "the angelic ones," *ta eidoliká* and *ta phantásmata*, "ghosts." The name *ta tsiniá*, "the false ones," occurs in Epirus. Such spirits are also often called euphemistically by other names, especially at night; thus, we hear of *ta 'pizelá*, "the enviable ones," on Tenos, *hoi kalótychoi*, "the fortunate ones," in Epirus, and "friends" or "brothers" in the region of Mount Parnassus.

It is still believed that these spirits are prone to visit certain localities, especially crossways, springs, caves, cemeteries, the vicinity of old mills and lonely trees, in general, places not frequently by men. In antiquity crossroads were places where frequently kings were buried and criminals executed, probably because rites and sacrifices were there made to the gods of the lower world. The Romans believed that Hecate and her dogs frequented such places, called *trivia* and *compita*, and they dedicated temples there to Diana, the *Trivia dea*. The *compita* were consecrated to the *Lares compitales*, the "spirits of the cross-roads," and in Italy were marked by shrines, where festivals called *"Compitalia"* were celebrated.

Such spirits are also believed nowadays to appear at certain times, notably at midnight and midday. Since moonlit nights are favorable to optical illusions, spirits are best seen at such times. One must not sing, whistle nor pipe at midnight as the spirits in this way are most easily assembled. However, they must all disappear at the third cock-crow. Noonday in Italy and Greece is also a favorable time for seeing spirits, since they assemble at that time while people stay indoors because of the heat and brilliancy of the sun, incidentally thus avoiding the malevolence of the dæmons, inflicted through sunstrokes, fevers, etc. Many modern peoples share with the Greeks and Italians this mystic awe of noonday. In late antiquity noon was regarded as the hour when the gods were pleased to visit their temples and rest, the time when men were away. According to Porphyry, at noonday the curtains were drawn in Greek temples and a sign placed over the door warning the people not to enter, since the gods were on a journey. Woe betide the man who dared to disturb them! Lucian says that at midday (and also at midnight) priests did not enter the holy grove of the Gauls near Marseilles, because they were fearful lest the gods might be there. Apollonius Rhodius has Jason behold the Libyan nymphs at noonday. Callimachus says that the youthful hunter Tiresias was surprised at noontide by Pallas as she bathed in the fountain of Hippocrene. Similarly Ovid has Actæon meet his doom when he sees Artemis and her maidens bathing at noontide. Theocritus' goatherd refuses to pipe at this hour because of dread of Pan, saying "I wot not high noon's his time for taking rest after the swink o' the chase." [30] Ovid has a shepherd pray to Pales that he meet not "the Dryads, nor Dian face to face, nor Taurus when at noon he walks abroad." [31] Schmidt long ago pointed out that this ancient superstition had influenced the *Septuagint* translators in rendering the words which appear in our version of the 91st Psalm as "the destruction that wasteth at noonday," so as to read, "destruction and noontide dæmon," thus referring to Pan.

In Greece to-day it is dangerous to loiter at noon around springs and fountains, or to lie under the shade of certain trees, such as the plane, poplar, fig, nut, or locust. In Crete one must not stand in the doorway at noon; if one does so, and sings or whistles, he is sure to lose his voice. At Arachova the flute must not be heard at midday, especially in summer. On Zante noon is the "heavy hour." On the top of Hymettus is a level space avoided by the shepherds at noon, since the Nereids are accustomed to dance there at that time. Leo Allatius alludes to the fear of the "daemon meridianus" on Chios in his day, the early seventeenth century. The Nereids on Zante have their dinner at midnight and must not be disturbed.

Certain seasons are chosen in preference to others by these supernatural beings for their appearance. On Zante they like to come on St. John's day; in Epirus they come in May, and elsewhere at the equinoxes and especially in the spring. During the twelve days' festival between Christmas and New Year's the spirits known as the Callicantzari are especially active.

The penalty meted out to those who disturb

the repose of a dæmon is called "the sudden."
Thus the phrase is often heard in Greece "the
sudden sickness has found him," and reminds
us of Plato's "sudden hour."

In the present chapter we shall discuss some
of the less malevolent types of these dæmons,
and shall begin with the Nereids, the most fa-
miliar and widespread of them all. Under
this name are no longer understood the beautiful sea-nymphs with mermaid bodies who used
to dwell in a resplendent cave in the depths of
the sea with their father Nereus, "the old man
of the sea." For Nereus, prophetic and propitious to sailors, no longer exists, nor any of
his fifty daughters, not even Amphitrite, the
wife of Poseidon, who was the "Lord of the
Ocean," for she has been replaced by the Lamia
of the Sea. Now the name Nereid has become
generalized and includes all that has survived
of the various nymphs,—whether those benevolent spirits who used to dwell on hill-tops
(Oreads), in groves and trees (Dryads), in
fresh water springs and fountains (Naiads),
or in Ocean stream (Oceanids and Nereids).
But all are nowadays indiscriminately called
Nereids, and the old word "nymph" has completely disappeared in the mythological sense,

and now is used only of a bride. Just as in the Homeric *Hymn to Aphrodite* lofty pines and oaks were the homes of the "deep-breasted mountain nymphs," and "men hew them not with the axe," so to-day no peasant will knowingly cut down a tree supposed to be haunted by a Nereid; if compelled to do so, he will take all needful precautions, such as praying to the Panaghia and making the sign of the cross, or lying prone on the ground in order not to see the spirit as it emerges. Otherwise he may be smitten dumb.

The Nereids now, like the ancient Naiads, protect many a mineral spring whose water is believed to be efficacious against disease. Such a spring may be roofed over like the one on Ithaca, described in the *Odyssey* as "a well-wrought flowing fountain," over which an altar was placed in honor of the nymphs, where the passer-by might make an offering. Pausanias describes a cavern near the river Anigrus in the western Peloponnesus sacred to the Anigridian Nymphs, whose "stinking" water was fatal to fishes and could cure lepers if they performed certain rites and swam in it. In Macedonia near the village of Cotzanes there is a spring in a grotto whose waters are believed to

issue from the breasts of the Nereids and to
cure all diseases. You enter with a lamp and
pitcher and fill both with water and leave bits
of clothing behind. You must not look back
as you return, else the water will not avail.
The old Corycian cave above Delphi, now
known as the *Sarantavli* or "Forty Chambers,"
which was formerly sacred to Pan and the
Nymphs, is still haunted by the Nereids. The
modern Nereids may be, after all, primarily
the representatives of the old Naiads, and the
modern word for water (*neró*) may, perhaps,
still echo their ancient frolic. They now tum-
ble and gamble in mill-streams and mountain
torrents, just as Nereus' daughters of old
sported in the waves of the sea.

There is one fundamental difference between
the ancient Nymphs and the present-day
Nereids. Whereas the former were benevolent guardians of the spots which they haunted,
the Nereids are generally regarded as malevolent and the peasants scrupulously avoid
them. In late antiquity, to be sure, the
Nymphs inspired awe in the peasants, as we
learn from Theocritus, who called them "the
dread goddesses of the country-folk." To pro-
pitiate them now they are frequently called by

euphemistic names, such as "the beautiful ladies," or, as on Parnassus, "our maidens." On Tenos and Myconus they are the "coast-dwellers," perhaps the nearest approach to the ancient daughters of Nereus. This idea of complimenting powers able to work harm to men is as rife to-day as it was in antiquity, when the Furies were called the *Eumenides*, "the kindly spirits."

The Nereids, like their prototypes, generally frequent lonely places, especially old mills, grottoes, and the dry beds of streams in summer. Many spots are now pointed out as their haunts. Thus a plateau on Parnassus is called the "Nereid Pits," and a spring on the same mountain is the "Nereid Spring." An entire mountain on Corfu is called the "Nereid Castle," while a cave containing a spring on Crete is known as the "Nereid Cave." We even hear of a village in Phthiotis named "Nereid." Certain cult spots once sacred to the Nymphs are now haunted by Nereids, as, *e. g.*, a small cave on the Hill of the Muses in Athens, and a rocky gorge in the bed of the Ismenus in Bœotia.

Like the fairies of Northern legend the Nereids are famed for their beauty and lovely

[143]

voices. They are imagined to be tall and slim and to have milk-white complexions and golden hair. They still are clothed in white and are adorned with garlands of flowers. Long veils are bound over their heads and shoulders, like those worn by Greek peasant women. Sometimes, as at Arachova, they carry the veil fluttering in the hand, just as we see them represented in ancient art, as in the Nereid Monument of Xanthus. Their preternatural beauty has given rise to many proverbial expressions. For a woman to be compared with a Nereid is a great compliment. Such phrases as, "She is as beautiful as a Nereid," "She has a Nereid's hair and eyes," "She sings and dances like a Nereid," are often heard. Fauriel has remarked that sometimes the Nereids have animal characteristics. Thus, in Maina they have goat-legs, like Pan, and dance on Mount Taÿgetus. If any one approaches them there, he is at first caressed and then dashed to pieces down the rocks. This is a reminiscence of the old Sirens, who in legend still sing in the neighborhood of Cape Malea and attract sailors from passing ships. On Zante the Nereids have the feet of an ass, and, in some places, even fish-tails like the mermaid Nereids of old.

They pass swiftly through the air and can easily disappear, sometimes becoming small enough to get through cracks and key-holes. In fact they can transform themselves into as many shapes as did Thetis in her mythical struggle with Peleus. Just as Chiron advised Peleus not to let go his prize until Thetis had resumed her original shape, so the same tactics must be used now to catch a Nereid.

As the old Nymphs enjoyed dancing and singing, hunting and a careless life generally, so the modern Nereids are light-hearted and given to song and dance. In a folk-song from Eubœa a Nereid is said to have danced until she died. They live mostly alone, but sometimes foregather to dance in some moonlit glade—on a threshing-floor, or, it may be, on the bright sands of some lonely island. At times, however, they can be serious, since they are trained in spinning and weaving, as in antiquity. Thus Pindar sang of the "Nereids with golden distaffs," and before him Homer mentions a weaving-room in the Nymphs' grotto on Ithaca sacred to the Naiads, where they wove purple garments. Virgil speaks of the Nymphs as spinning Milesian fleeces. A creeping plant around a tree is now called

"Nereid yarn," and on Zante and Cephalonia stones with holes in them are called "Nereid spindles," and, if small enough, are hung round children's necks to protect them from the Nereids. On Zante they are believed to be industrious, for they visit houses before morning and complete the weaving left unfinished by the housewife.

On Zante they have a leader, as Artemis led the Nymphs in ancient lore, and this leader is the most beautiful of all. In Elis a Lamia is their leader. Often they are represented as married to devils, and hence are often called "she-devils." On Parnassus their husbands may be heard by the peasants playing on musical instruments and dancing in grottoes, such as the Corycian cave. Frequently they gather around a piping shepherd and begin to dance to his music. They are long-lived, but not immortal, and many stories tell of their death by lightning or at the hands of mortals. Just so in the Homeric *Hymn to Aphrodite*, the Nymphs are midway between mortals and immortals, eating heavenly food and dancing with the gods, but still fated to die. The Nereids often fall in love with handsome youths, whom they reward with prosperity. If such a favorite, however, slights his Nereid love, he is sure to meet dire misfortune,—blindness, dumbness, insanity, or even death. Especially is loss of voice feared by him who accosts them, which recalls the similar notion regarding fairies held in Shakespeare's day. Thus Falstaff says: "he that speaks to them, shall die." On the other hand, sometimes men fall in love with them and ensnare them into becoming their wives. Many stories are told of such marriages, and families descended from Nereids are pointed out here and there in Greece and are greatly esteemed. Thus the great Revolutionary family of Maina, Mavromichales, claims Nereid blood. Kampouroglu [32] speaks of such a family in the Attic village of Menidhi, and Schmidt talked with a peasant in the village of Mariais on Zante who made the same claim. At Distomo, at the foot of Mount Cirphis opposite Delphi, there are two families who are said to be descended from a Nereid union, and their men and women are said to be very beautiful. Similarly, in antiquity many noble Athenian families traced their descent from nymphs.

If a mortal can steal and hide a Nereid's veil, she loses her power of transformation and has to follow the man to his home. Such wives, however, soon lose their merry ways and become morose. If they find their veils, they run away. They cannot return to their sisters, but must live alone thereafter as the guardians of springs and fountains. Sometimes it is the possession of a ring which puts a Nereid in a mortal's power. Schmidt tells a story to the effect that two hundred years before his visit to Zante a man from Mariais was seized by the Nereids and made to dance with them. He succeeded in getting a ring from one of them and she was obliged to follow him home. Two boys and a girl were the fruit of the union. One day the Nereid found the hidden ring and ran away taking with her one boy and one-half of her daughter. The peasant with whom Schmidt conversed, as claiming Nereid blood, was descended from the surviving boy. A more famous story about a Nereid marriage comes from Crete, which recalls the marriage of Peleus and Thetis, as here the Nereid transformed herself successively into a dog, a snake, a camel, and fire, but to no avail.

The Nereids punish those who watch their dances and who try to speak to them. Such people generally become dumb or waste away.

Children so affected are "struck by the Nereids" and are called *nympholeptais*. Nympholepsy, the condition of being "possessed by the Nymphs," was the name in antiquity for all sorts of mental disturbances,—poetic rapture, prophetic frenzy, and insanity. Whoever was possessed, suffered depression and strange fits of frenzy and desired solitude. Nowadays if a man be caught beside a spring or under a tree where a Nereid is resting, he may become a *nymphóleptos*. Bent visited a cave on Siphnus over which were inscribed the words "Sanctuary of the Nymphs," and he records that travelers who crossed a stream nearby at midday or midnight might become possessed by the Nereids. To be cured they had to place at a neighboring crossroads or hang on the wall of the cave a piece of bread wrapped in a napkin along with an offering of honey, milk, and eggs. A tendency to melancholy and solitude is also nowadays ascribed to the influence of the Nereids. Ross [33] recounts a story from Chalandri in Attica which he heard in 1833. The wife of the village priest was in great sorrow, because the Nereids had decoyed away her twelve-year old daughter, who frequently left her home and visited

[149]

the foothills of the neighboring Mount Bri-
lessus, where for many days at a time she wandered alone in the early morning or late at
night. The priest prayed in vain to the Virgin,
as finally the child died. Neighbors claimed to
have seen her dancing with the Nereids only
two days before her death.

The Nereids are especially jealous of married
women and mothers. Such women wear amulets and place garlic over their house-doors for
protection. Sometimes a cross is painted on
the lintel, and if there be a knock on the door
at night, it is not answered. As the Nereids
have a propensity to carry off new-born babes,
or to leave changelings in their place, great
precautions are taken at births. On Rhodes
for forty days after a birth the house-door is
bolted at night. In the country parts of Greece
children are carried by their mothers with them
into the fields for protection. Sometimes a
stolen child will be returned more beautiful.
The Nereids often draw children down into
springs, just as the old Naiads entwined their
arms about the ill-fated Hylas as he went to
fetch water and drew him down.

Injuries inflicted by the Nereids are not
permanent, but may be cured by prayer, by

incantations, and by offerings of milk, honey, and cakes placed in spots haunted by them. A Greek writer [34] tells of honey cakes being placed in a cave at Athens in 1818 by a man and a woman, who then ran away without looking back. Schmidt says that on Zante candy and sweetmeats were offered in his day at crossroads. Theocritus has Lacon tell Comatas that he will dedicate a great bowl of milk to the nymphs. On Corfu, milk and honey are offered to avert whirlwinds, which are there ascribed to the agency of the Nereids. If one fails to crouch during such a storm, especially during the passing of the *anemostróvilos*, he will be lifted off his feet by the Nereids. On Zante at such times the peasants believe that the Nereids are dancing. Thus, the modern Nereids are frequently confused with the ancient storm-spirits, the Harpies, who in the *Odyssey* carry off Pandareus' daughters in a storm, and by whom Penelope prayed that she might be borne away in order to avoid her hard plight.

The modern Greeks believe in local protecting spirits or guardians everywhere. Just as every spot in antiquity—every grove, fountain, garden, gorge, etc.—had its tutelary *genius*, its nymph, Pan, or Priapus, so now every such place has its *stoicheion,* which is a word of ancient lineage. Plato called the four primary substances of the earlier philosophers—fire, water, earth, and air—*stoicheia.* The Neo-Platonists transferred the term from these physical elements to the spirits which were believed to animate them. St. Paul refers to the "elements of the world"; in one passage he asks: "how turn ye again to the weak and beggarly elements, whereunto ye desire again to be in bondage?" [35] Here the word "elements" (in the *Revised Version,* "rudiments") should be translated "spirits," in order to give the personal meaning of the Greek. The ordinary man identified these spirits, in general, with the local genii which were supposed to haunt all parts of the visible world, and this popularization of the term, *stoicheia,* has been kept up by the Eastern Church. In Greece the Nereids, the Lamias, and many other supernatural beings are, in a sense, such *genii.* But we shall follow the five-fold division of these spirits made by Lawson, according to their place of dwelling: the *genii* of buildings, who haunt houses, churches, bridges, etc.; those of water, who inhabit springs and rivers; terrestrial spirits, who inhabit mountains and caves; the spirits of the air; and, lastly, the guardian angels, good and bad, of men. The latter class we shall leave for our last chapter, and consider the other four in the present connection.

The most frequent of all such genii are the house-spirits, which are recognized everywhere in Greece, even among the Albanians and Vlachs. Thus it is a universal belief that a *genius loci* lives under every house in the form of a dog, a cat, a pig, or, most commonly, a snake. Without such a guardian the house cannot stand. If a house is destroyed, the snake will seek another. Schmidt recounts the story of a wealthy Greek peasant who built a fine house. One day he found one of his children in the garden playing with a snake, which was licking the child's hand and curling around its feet. Horror-struck he frightened the snake away. Next day it was found nearly dead from fright and was killed and thrown away. Immediately the house fell in. On Zante bread-crumbs are sprinkled over a crevice through which the snake is supposed to enter the house. When families assemble, especially during the Christmas festival, the house-snake is not forgotten. On New Year's eve it has its

[153]

share of St. Basil's cake, an offering which plays a great rôle in Macedonia. The cake is set on the center of the table and incense is shaken over it; then it is cut up by the parents, one part being set apart for St. Basil, another for the house-spirit, a third for the domestic animals, a fourth for the furniture, and the rest for the members of the family. After supper the table is placed in the corner for St. Basil, in order that he may share in the cake. On Cyprus, the first plate at dinner, a cup of wine, and a purse of money are set upon the table for the house-spirit. On Chios, on New Year's day, a mixture of beans, currants, and pomegranate seeds is made; one of the household must sleep elsewhere and return next day, when he sprinkles the concoction over the house and its inmates. On Samos and on the Ionian Islands water vessels are filled at night and left standing for the house-spirit. In antiquity great reverence was paid to such spirits. Thus Theophrastus has the superstitious man erect a shrine, if he sees a snake in the house. One Xenocrates wrote a book on domestic divination, in which he devoted a division to the house-snake. The snake was always the emblem of the chthonian deities, and to-day the belief in the house-snake is descended from such worship.

The house-spirit is propitiated by a regular ceremony, which has its origin in human sacrifice. When ground is cleared for a new structure, a "foundation sacrifice" takes place. When the owner's family and workmen are gathered together, a priest takes holy water and blesses the spot. Then an animal, a fowl, lamb, or goat, is slain and its blood sprinkled over the foundation stone and its body buried beneath, on the theory that the blood gives stability to the foundation. Sometimes it is the shadow of an animal that is so utilized. Miss Hamilton records that on Samos a bird or a lamb is brought to the site of the foundation stone and so placed that its shadow may fall upon it. Over this shadow the first stone is then laid. Later the animal is killed and buried elsewhere. She also recounts how on Lesbos the natives avail themselves of the shadow of a passer-by who is entrapped with hypocritical friendliness, or the builder may even cast a stone at it. Within the year the passer-by will die and become the *genius* of the building. Sometimes the builder will secretly measure a man's shadow and bury the measure beneath the foundations, and then also the man will die within the year. This reflects the ancient Greek idea that a man's shadow represented his soul and that its loss meant death. Thus Pausanias mentions a precinct of Zeus on Mount Lycæus into which no creature, whether man or beast, could enter with safety, for it would lose its shadow and die within the year. Theopompus also states that people who entered the precinct lost their shadow, and Plutarch adds that if they did so intentionally they were stoned to death, but if unintentionally they were merely sent away to the village of Eleutheræ. So in Greece to-day the shadow is believed to be a vital part of a man and its loss fatal. The "foundation sacrifice," then, is really a survival of human sacrifice. The slain animal, the shadow, or even the burial of a portion of a man's clothing are merely more civilized substitutes for human sacrifice. On Zante, Schmidt found the belief still current that it is best to ensure the strength of a fort or a bridge by slaying and burying a man upon the spot. A monk told him that it was merely the fear of the law which kept the people from carrying out the idea. Such a man, however, must not be a Christian, but a Jew or a Moslem.

Human sacrifice is proved by many legends about Eastern bridges, showing that such an act was considered essential to the safety of the structure. The best known legend of the kind is connected with the lofty single-arched bridge of Arta near the Ambracian Gulf, where the *genius* of the bridge, *i. e.*, of the river below, exacted the usual cruel toll, similar to that exacted by the ancient river-gods. When the forty-five master-builders and the sixty laborers had toiled in vain for three years to hang the arch—for it fell each night—the master-mason had a dream in which he was told:

"If you slay not a human life, the walls can ne'er
  be founded;
No nobleman it be, nor serf, nor any 'neath the
  heavens;
But e'en the master-mason's wife, his wife must
  be the victim." [36]

So he hypocritically summons his beautiful wife to come dressed in festal array, and tells her that his wedding-ring has fallen beside the arch, and that she alone can recover it. She descends into the excavation and is immediately buried by the workmen in stone and mortar. Then the arch is spanned.

Water genii still haunt fountains and rivers. They are sometimes imagined as having the forms of dragons or bulls, like the old river-gods, but more frequently they appear as the Black Giant, a monster of Oriental origin, frequently called an "Arab." It may be that the Arab slaves, who were the inmates of most households in Turkish times, were suspected by their Christian masters of being in league with the Devil, and hence were metamorphosed into such genii. These "Arabs" have the power to assume any shape they wish. It depends upon them whether the water of a well or fountain is healthful to drink. Schmidt found a spring on Myconus, where the water had to be greeted three times before it was drunk, in order to appease its spirit. At the spring of St. Symeon near Steiri on Parnassus a cannibal "Arab" is believed to guard a rich treasure. Often he is heard in the village as he takes his delight in playing with his gold pieces. At another spring on Chios a monster named Venias dwells, who leaves his abode at midnight and rides on a wild horse through the village street and again disappears in the fountain. Whoever drinks of his water becomes foolish or insane. Such giants frequently fight; thus two of them, who live in Kastri (Delphi) and Arachova respectively, villages twelve miles apart, fight at a spring near the latter town. If the Arachovite wins, the Kastriotes die, and vice versa. Above, on the top of Parnassus, such giants also contend. From such battles the Arachovites fancy that cold weather and snow-storms come, which belief shows a confusion between these genii and the old gods of the winds, just as we saw that at times the present Nereids are confused with the old Harpies. Such fountain "Arabs" are generally harmless, although they are fond of inveigling beautiful maidens by seductive promises to their palaces beneath the waters. In Crete, Rodd found that such spirits, there known as "Saracens," were called on by mothers as bogies by which to frighten their naughty children.

The terrestrial genius, who inhabits mountain caves, gorges, clefts, and other desolate spots, is generally known as the Dracus or Dracondas, and is one of the commonest of these *stoicheia*. Since at times the Dracus is also conceived as haunting wells and springs, he is closely related to the Black Giant just discussed. Unlike the latter, however, the Dracus is generally malevolent. He often appears as a big snake or as a monster having the body of a snake and the head of a man. Von Hahn tells of one in Maina which had seven heads and the power of form-shifting. In many legends the Dracus guards treasure, just as the Colchian dragon guarded the Golden Fleece from the Argonauts and the guardian-dragon watched over the apples in the Garden of the Hesperides. If a man dreams of buried treasure, he must say nothing about it, but go at once to the spot indicated and sacrifice a dog, a sheep, or a goat, in order to appease the dragon. Then only can he dig it up. But if he tells any one his dream, or forgets to sacrifice, he will find that the treasure has been turned to ashes. In his *Oneirocritica*, Artemidorus says that a dream about dragons "signifies riches and wealth, since the dragon dwells over treasures."

In many folk-tales the Dracus figures as a large and uncouth human monster, like the Giants of our fairy-tales. In fact, such stories provide the usual hero of Greek fairy-tales.

But he is easily outwitted and possesses none of the subtlety of our Devil nor of the clever Mohammedan *Ifrit*. His similarity to the Teutonic Giant is also shown by the fact that the Dracus can perform great feats of strength. As we hear of the Giants' Causeway in Ireland, we hear of a great stone known as the "Dracus' Weight," south of the village of Negrita in Macedonia; nearby is a mound called "Dracus' Shovelful," and a rock in the same neighborhood is known as "Dracus' Tomb." Near the village of Liaccovicia in the plain of Serres two solitary rocks are called "Dracus' Quoits." Many caves in Greece are known as the "Dragon's Caves," for we find them on the islands of Zante, Cephalonia, and Astypalæa, and on Parnassus and elsewhere. The Dracus sometimes has a spouse—Dracæna or Dracondissa, who is as big and foolish as her husband. In the Eastern Church, saints slay such dragons, just as heroes slew them in antiquity.[37]

Dæmons of the air have been believed in by the Greeks from the time of Hesiod to the present day. But with Hesiod they were the benevolent spirits of men who had lived in the Golden Age. Now they are no longer beneficent, but as hostile to man as most of the other

supernatural spirits by whom he is encom-
passed. As a whole, this class of dæmons is too
vague in the popular imagination to be clearly
defined, so we shall confine our attention
briefly to only one division of such air-spirits,
a species which has an acknowledged province
of authority, the so-called *Telonia*. These are
spirits which hover between earth and heaven
and interfere with the passage of the soul to
heaven. Between them and the angels an end-
less strife is supposed to be waged, the *telonia*
hindering, the angels hastening the advent of
the soul before God. The name, which is a
diminutive of the word *telones*, a "publican"
or "toll-gatherer," means "toll-houses." The
naïve Greek idea seems to be that the soul on
its way upwards is embarrassed by aërial cus-
tom-houses, just as the body was embarrassed
here on its journey through life. This may explain—as we shall note in the final chapter—
the custom once common among the modern
Greeks of placing a coin in the mouth of the
dead man, not as a ferry-charge for Charus, but
as a toll for the Telonia. The words of Jesus
found in Luke [38] have been appealed to by
Greek commentators as referring to these spirits: "Thou fool, this night thy soul shall be re-

quired of thee." Here the Greek reads, "they require thy soul," where the vague plural has been explained as referring to the *Telonia*. Certain illnesses are due to the malignity of these spirits, and also certain night phenomena, such as comets and meteors, are believed to be manifestations of them. They are greatly dreaded by sailors, to whom St. Elmo's light, the flame which flickers around the masts and yards on stormy nights, is a manifestation of their hostility. Sailors invoke the aid of the saints against them by firing guns, or by sticking black-handled knives into the masts. In antiquity the appearance of two such lights was, on the contrary, regarded as the sign of the good spirits, Castor and Pollux, whom Horace apostrophized as the *"fratres Helenae, lucida sidera,"* and who were believed to save storm-bound sailors.

Traditions, which go back to the Titans, Giants, and Cyclopes, have been found here and there in Greece, especially on the Ionian Islands. On Zante Schmidt found the tradition of giants with long beards and one eye in their foreheads which sparkled like fire, recalling Virgil's description of Cyclops' "huge eye, that lay deep-set beneath his savage brow,

like an Argive shield or the lamp of Phœbus."
The father of such monsters is now believed to
have been a devil, who, mated to a Lamia or
a sorceress, created their race. They dwell
within the earth, and spend their time lifting
large stones and building them into fortresses.
Their wives are equally large and ply great
distaffs. In a former war against a certain
king, these women slew thousands of the
enemy by hurling their distaffs at them. Such
giants cause earthquakes, showing that originally they were personifications of natural disturbances like the old Giants in the legend of
the *Gigantomachy*. Another belief on Zante is
that they have been imprisoned by God against
their will; for they once rebelled against his
rule and were vanquished by his thunderbolts.
This is surely a reminiscence of the old battle
between Zeus and the Titans. There has also
been found a reminiscence of the legend of
Achilles in the stories about these present-day
giants. For they are vulnerable only in the
ankle-bone, since their mother after their birth
baptized them in a river, leaving only the foot-
joint unwetted. There are also reminders of
such Cyclopes outside the island of Zante.
Thus the Arachovites say that in some strange

land there exists a race of godless men who have only one eye in their forehead. This legend recalls Strabo's race of "one-eyed Cyclopes." In fact the Arachovites use the term as one of reproach, calling any savage-tempered man "one-eyed." Among the Acarnanians, the Xeromerites call their hated neighbors, the Baltines, a savage mountain tribe, "one-eyed." A sailor story from the isle of Psaria, recorded by Ross,[39] recalls the story of Odysseus and Polyphemus. The hero of the story is rescued from the clutches of a blind cannibal dragon in a way which is somewhat similar to that by which Odysseus escapes from the cave of the blinded Cyclops. He hides in the skin of a ram which he has slain, and on all fours creeps by the watchful dragon.

During the twelve days between Christmas and Epiphany supernatural beings are believed to be especially active. Among these are the Callicantzari, who are among the best known sprites of modern Greek superstition. Although the name has many dialectical variations and the forms assumed by these spirits vary in different parts, the time of their appearance and their general characterisics are uniform. While Schmidt argued that the name

[165]

was of Turkish origin, and reached the Greeks by way of the Albanians, later students of folk-lore, such as Lawson and Polites, have concluded that the Turks borrowed it from the Greeks. These dæmons have been divided into two classes, one, the larger variety, ranging in size from that of a man to that of a giant, the other, mere hobgoblins of pigmy dimensions. Whereas the former are malicious and even deadly, the smaller are generally harmless, haunting the cabins of the peasants and merely annoying their inmates by frolicsome pranks. The latter are not feared by the people and may, therefore, be merely a later development of the original larger type.

The larger Callicantzari are usually black and have hairy bodies, big heads, black or red faces, bloodshot eyes, blood-red tongues, ears of goats or asses, and fierce tusks. They are very lean and have the arms and hands of monkeys, their long nails being curved like vultures' talons. Their tails are long and they often have curious legs, one of them that of an animal, such as an ass or goat, the other of a man, but with the feet distorted. Though lame they are very swift. The smaller variety, generally human in form, has curious characteristics. Thus the Arachovites regard them as pygmies who ride through their streets in great numbers on Christmas night in a droll procession—one being mounted on a cock with his legs trailing, another on a dog-sized horse, another on a huge donkey, and still others on lame or one-eyed or one-eared animals. Here they frequently are one-eyed themselves, or blind, or they squint, their features also being askew. Their leader has a very large head and a very small mouth from which the tongue protrudes. He keeps the rest of the cavalcade in order with his shouts. Some carry musical instruments and others large dry pumpkins, which are thrown to the ground with resounding thumps.

The Callicantzari are generally regarded as stupid and quarrelsome. They roam at night, but, like all spirits, disappear at the third cock-crow. Then they return beneath the earth, where they dwell with their wives feeding on snakes, toads, and lizards, and spend their time trying to saw through the great tree on which the earth is supposed to stand. During their absence above ground the tree grows again so that their labor is in vain. They knock at doors or descend the chimney and defile the pots and pans, the furniture, the food, and especially the wells. Again they disturb the peasants' slumber by throwing bricks down the chimney or by making unearthly noises. When they enter a house they sit on the chests of the inmates and frighten them nearly to death. Hideous to look upon, they increase their ugliness by keeping themselves unkempt or dressed in rags. They excrete defilement through their noses and mouths. Like the "Arabs" they lust after women, whom they carry off to their caves.

They may be scared off by pagan magic and by certain Christian rites. Among the former methods, fire is chief. So the hearth-fire is kept merrily burning during the twelve days of their appearance, and bonfires are common. Or a burning faggot may be laid before the house-door and people out at night may carry firebrands with them. At Arachova, the drinking pots defiled by them are cleansed with hot coals, and polluted wells are purified either by casting such coals into them or by placing burnt sticks over them. In Leo Allatius' day more drastic methods were used. Children born on Christmas Eve were then brought into the market-place of the village and had their

feet singed in a big bonfire and were later
anointed with oil.   In this way the child's po-
tential talons were destroyed—the talons being the most characteristic part of a Callicantzarus.   Cakes also appease them nowadays, as
they do all classes of spirits.   At Melanik in
Macedonia, Abbott relates how the peasants
scald the Callicantzarus on New Year's Eve.
The housewife makes cakes within, while her
husband stands outside dressed in a fur-coat
turned wrong side out, and dances and sings
these words:

> "I *am a Skantzos, even as thou art one,*
>   *Come, then, let us dance together*
>   *And let us moisten the pastry.*" [40]

This song is continued until the man hears the
syrup hiss as it is poured over the cakes, a
sound symbolic of the scalding of these mis-
chievous sprites.   On Zante and Chios a sieve
is often placed upon the hearth.   The Callicantzarus, on descending the chimney, stops to
count the holes in the sieve, but as he can
never reach the Christian number three, he is
overtaken by dawn, and thus his arithmetical
passion proves his undoing.   In Macedonia,
mustard or millet seeds are scattered over the

roof or tomb of a vampire, since the vampire cannot leave his tomb nor enter a house until he has counted them. Herbs are also hung over the chimney-piece or door to scare the Callicantzari away. They can be appeased by offerings of pork, their favorite food. Rodd recounts the story of a woman on Spetsa who, with two others, went to gather firewood on the far side of the island near a cave on the shore. Soon she disappeared and days later was found seated upon a rock, and was rescued by sailors in a boat. She remained dumb until taken to church, where the spirit was exorcised, and finally she regained her speech, and told how the Callicantzari had carried her off.

As for Christian methods of driving them away, we may mention that on Epiphany eve, the last night that they are out, the priest visits each house and marks a cross on the door or on the kitchen utensils which the Callicantzari defile. The housewife guides him around, as he pours holy water into every corner, and blesses the well and reads the office over a bowl of holy water, dipping the cross with a bunch of basil into it, with which he besprinkles

[170]

the house. Instead of the old Chiote ordeal by fire already mentioned, nowadays children, who have been born in this period of twelve days, are merely baptized. And no marriage is supposed to be solemnized then. On Zante those born on Christmas Day or Eve are now believed to become Callicantzari, which means that they may have been conceived at the festival of the "Annunciation of the Virgin" on March 25; such conception is regarded as a sin and a child so born is its punishment. Near the town of Zante, Schmidt saw a peasant whom the townsfolk regarded as a Callicantzarus. Sometimes the Christian exorcism is not sufficient, and a house where these spirits elect to remain becomes haunted and must be deserted.

All sorts of explanations of the origin of these curious spirits have been offered, a few of which we shall briefly notice.

The Greeks themselves believe that the larger, malevolent variety comes from the disembodied souls of those who have met a violent death or had no funeral rites, and hence, like the vampires, or like the souls of the unburied in ancient times, roam about their old haunts for revenge. They regard the mis-

chievous smaller variety as the ghosts of ancestors who still linger and watch over the welfare of their old homes—a sort of degraded
Manes or Lares. Lawson, by ingenious reasoning, has tried to trace the Callicantzari back
to the old Centaurs, not to the typical hippo-
centaurs of Greek art and legend, but to another related species of mixture of men and
animals, especially the Satyrs. He points out
that on Macedonian coins a Satyr sometimes is
represented with a horse's hoofs, ears, and tail;
and Miss Harrison has shown that Centaur and
Satyr are merely different types of the horse-
man. Although the name "Satyr" is no longer
heard, Lawson contends that the genus has survived in the Callicantzarus. By the beginning
of the Christian era the word "Centaur" com-
prised several species of monsters half-man
and half-beast, horse-centaurs, ass-centaurs,
Satyrs and Sileni, each of which species con-
tributed to the modern Callicantzarus—the
horse-centaur least and the ass-centaur and the
Satyr most. Satyrs and Sileni were the ordinary companions of Dionysus, and consequently the Callicantzari are the modern representatives of the associates of the Wine-god.
He bases his theory on the supposed etymology

of the word and on the mixed state and character of the present spirits.

Long before, Schmidt had concluded that the night-roaming, the brutality, the sharp claws and teeth, and the form-shifting of the larger type were derived from the were-wolf, which, as we shall see, was a well-known superstition in ancient Greece. He pointed out that the Turkish name *Kara-kond-jolos* meant were-wolf, and that, outside of Greece, the were-wolf appeared only at Christmas time. Similarly, Abbott has referred the Callicantzari to a species of were-wolf akin to the modern Greek vampire, which is largely a survival of the ancient belief in lycanthropy. Rodd also thinks that the belief that children born at this season may become Callicantzari and grow tiger-like claws with which they tear and frighten those whom they meet, may point to the were-wolf origin of these dæmons. Miss Hamilton, on the other hand, believes that the Callicantzari are merely the counterpart of the masqueraders who figured so prominently in the Græco-Roman festivals, and who still appear at the Carnival. At Christmas time in Greece to-day parties go from house to house with grotesque masks and jangling bells.

It may be that the fear inspired by such masks caused the belief in the demoniacal nature of these spirits. But the old explanation of Leo Allatius goes back farther than all, in tracing the origin of the Callicantzari and their ancient prototype as well, in maintaining that these spirits are merely the result of nightmares caused by indigestion following the feasting indulged in at Christmas time; for, as he pointed out, these spirits have characteristics of nightmares—night-roaming, jumping on the shoulders and sitting on the chests of men, and leaving them senseless with fear.

VI.   DÆMONOLOGY: LAMIAS, VAMPIRES, AND WERE-WOLVES

WE NOW turn to a more malevolent class of supernatural spirits, those characterized by their lust for human blood.   In the Middle Ages these were confused in the popular imagination because of their common propensity to prey upon children.   But we shall find that they are distinct species of supernatural powers, and go back to well-known ancient prototypes.   We shall here discuss only the more important of these malevolent dæmons—the Lamias, vampires, and were-wolves.

Traces can still be found in Greece of the Lamias, the fabulous monsters, who, by their voluptuous arts, enticed young men to their doom, longing for their blood.   The old name, Lamia, now more commonly spelled Lamna and Lamnissa, and the old characteristics reappear in many legends.   The name is applied sometimes to one being, and again, as in later antiquity, to a class of beings. They now appear as both land and water spirits. Thus we hear of a sea-power named Lamia, related to the old Nereids; for in Elis she is the queen of the present Nereids, and elsewhere has replaced Amphitrite, the wife of Poseidon. Nowadays she is hostile to sailors, against whom she arouses the storm-wind. Schmidt found a pretty legend of this "shore Lamia" on the northern coast of the Corinthian Gulf near Itea. There, if a man plays his flute at midday or midnight a Lamia comes up out of the water and invites him to be her husband; if he refuses, she may kill him for the slight. Here they have the characteristics of the old sirens, who used to lure storm-bound sailors to their doom, for, under the hope of rescue, sailors blindly follow the ever receding voices of the Lamias. Passow gives a pretty folk-song from the region around Salonica, in which the shepherd Gianes plays his flute on the shore, despite many warnings of his mother. At last the Lamia appears and lays a wager that if he tires her dancing by his music she will become his wife, but if she tires him piping, he will forfeit his flocks. Gianes plays uninterruptedly for three days and nights until he has to stop through sheer weariness and so loses his sheep and goats.

More commonly, however, the Lamias are land spirits and have cannibal characteristics which are especially dangerous to children, an idea which is chiefly derived from antiquity. In this form they are hideous monsters, having the forms of gigantic women with deformed limbs, their feet being represented as dissimilar or three in number, one being that of an ox, an ass, or a goat. On Corfu and Zante many stories are told of their voracity, and hence 'to eat like a Lamia" is proverbial. But, for the most part, they have ceased to inspire fear in the country-folk, and like their counterparts in antiquity, the Lamia, Empousa, and Mormo, are merely bug-bears by which mothers frighten their naughty children. When a child dies suddenly, it is said the "Lamia has strangled it." The name is also used of a scolding woman. But, curiously enough, in Arachova the Lamia, by some subtle alchemy, has been changed into a good spirit, a beautiful woman, tall and graceful, who used to be seen at dusk striding through the streets of the town or seated by a fountain just outside, distaff in hand. This may be a lingering memory of the Lamia who in antiquity dwelt in a cave high up on the opposite Mount Cirphis and ravaged the countryside until she was slain by a hero. And here in Arachova handsome maidens are likened to Lamias, just as elsewhere in Greece they are likened to Nereids.

Despite her propensity to gluttony and blood, the modern Lamia is of noble lineage. The original Lamia, as recounted by Diodorus and others, was a beautiful queen of Libya whose beauty attracted the fatal love of Zeus himself. The result of his admiration was a number of lovely children of which the jealous Hera deprived her. Thereafter the mother hid among the rocks and caverns of the sea, where her beauty was turned into ugliness and her goodness into malevolence. In order to console herself for her loss, she began at first to steal the children of others, and then to afflict them with wasting disease or to kill them outright. To spite Hera, Zeus gave her the power to take her eyes out and put them in again, in this way adding terror to her brutality and lust. Finally she also attacked old men and women, and, like a sinister vampire, sucked their blood. But by the time of Aristophanes the Lamia had become the joke of the comic stage, and throughout late antiquity she figured mostly in nursery legends as an ugly woman of great size, ignorant of housewifely arts, as at present. In later times the Lamias were pictured as lying in wait along the roadside for youths rather than children, and they were able to change themselves into any shape in order better to get their prey, whose heart-blood they were eager to suck. Then they took on the attractive forms of young maidens, though, when not disguised, they resumed their usual forms, their bodies ending in the tails of serpents, being blood-stained and their women's faces red. This vampire type of Lamia, as described by Philostratus, was at the base of Keats' famous poem.

The most repulsive of Greek popular superstitions is the belief in the vampire, known generally on the mainland by the Slavic name *vrykólakas* or *vourkólakas*. Although education and the Church have succeeded in reducing this monstrous belief, it is still to be found among the Greek peasantry.

A Greek vampire is not a disembodied spirit, like the dæmons which we have so far discussed, but an undissolved body or reanimated corpse, which for some reason cannot rest in

[179]

the grave, and consequently rises at times and roams about the earth preying on living men. By feeding on human blood it renews its vitality, and hence is actuated by murderous impulses. Leo Allatius says that in his day, when the belief was far stronger than it is now, it was believed that the devil got into the corpses of the wicked and excommunicated, which became swollen, and the joints could not be bent. He says that they issued at night and roamed about knocking at the doors of houses. Whoever answered the knock, was sure to die next day; but since they never knocked twice, those within never answered a first call. Nowadays a vampire may be abroad in daylight, but generally only from a couple of hours before midnight until cockcrow. In any case he must return to his grave at least once a week, on Saturday according to Greek belief, on Friday or Saturday according to Albanian.

It is the custom among Greeks and Orthodox Albanians to exhume the body of a relative at the end of three years in order to discover if it has properly decomposed. The Greek Church officially recognizes this custom by the petition read at the burial service, "dissolve into thy component elements." If the body be found to be dissolved, the bones are washed in wine, and are carried in an ossuary to the church where they are left for nine days. This may be in part a reminiscence of the old custom, noted already in the *Iliad*, of extinguishing the funeral pyre with wine and collecting the bones after cremation into a cinerary urn. After the nine days have passed, the bones are either reburied in the former grave or cast into the charnel-house of the church. But if the body is not dissolved, the soul is not at rest, and the corpse becomes a *vrykólakas*. In order to be sure that it has decomposed, the same exhumation ceremony is repeated three years later. The worst Greek curse is: "May the earth not eat thee," *i. e.*, "May you become a vampire." Vampirism is supposed to be hereditary in certain families, which are consequently shunned by their neighbors. The Romaic poet Valorites, in a very realistic poem, has described the rousing from their graves of the wicked Ali Pasha and his Greek lieutenant Thanase Vaghia by the vampires of the inhabitants of Gardici, who had been massacred by them. Perhaps the best Greek vampire story is one from Crete long ago related by Pashley.[41]

The Church sanctioned the superstition in the early centuries, although it has made strenuous efforts since to root it out. It used to cite in its defence the words of Jesus to his disciples, in Matthew: "Whatsoever ye shall bind on earth, shall be bound in heaven; and whatsoever ye shall loose on earth, shall be loosed in heaven." This was supposed by some to mean that the incorruptibility of a man's body would follow, if it were bound by a curse. The apostles passed the power on to the bishops who could bind or loose, *i. e.,* stop or hasten the decay of the body. When to-day a vampire is abroad, the priest reads a part of the ritual at the suspected grave. If this proves inadequate, the grave is opened and the body exposed and exorcised. It should then forthwith fall to ashes. In extreme cases a stake or nail is driven into the heart, or the latter is torn out and boiled in oil or vinegar, or again the whole body is hacked and burnt. Leake— who says that in his day it was difficult to meet with an example of the superstition—tells of the belief once prevalent in Epirus that the devil enters the *vourkólakas,* who rises from the grave and torments his relatives and others, killing them or causing them to sicken. He says that then the remedy was "to dig up the body, and if, after it has been exorcised by the priest, the dæmon still persists in annoying the living, to cut the body into small pieces, or, if that be not sufficient, to burn it." [42] Abbott tells of just such a ceremony at Alistrati in Macedonia, a village between Serres and Drama, where the corpse of a suspected vampire was exhumed and scalded in oil and pierced through the navel with a long nail. The tomb was then closed and millet scattered over it, that the vampire, if he should return, might waste his time in counting the grains and thus be overtaken by daylight. De Tournefort,[43] the French traveler, in 1701 was an eye-witness of the destruction of a vampire on the island of Myconus. He tells with all the gruesome details how the body was finally transferred to the neighboring island of St. George, and there, after mass in the chapel had been said, the heart was cut out and buried, and later, since the apparition continued, the entire body was burned to ashes. The island of Hydria was formerly infested with these monsters, until finally a friendly bishop transferred them to the unoccupied isle of Therasia in the Santorin group, where they still roam at night, but can do no harm, as they cannot cross the salt water to their old haunts. "To send vampires to Santorin," is said to be as common a proverb among the islands of the Ægean, as "to send owls to Athens" was throughout ancient Greece.

The civil authorities in various places have been instrumental in curtailing the superstition. Long ago the Venetians in the Ionian islands demanded proofs before allowing suspected bodies to be exhumed and the resort made to more extreme measures. The Turks also tried to suppress atrocities connected with exterminating suspected vampires on the Ægean islands, where the superstition used to be particularly rife. But despite ecclesiastical and civil attempts to rout it out, the ghastly superstition is strong in some parts of Greece even yet. Polites tells of the burning of a vampire near Patras as late as 1902.

Various causes of vampirism have been adduced. Those who have been excommunicated by the Church, those convicted of great crimes, and those dying under a curse or by suicide are believed to become vampires. On Cephalonia the offspring of a marriage between a woman and a god-father (*koumbáros*) may become one. In Maina the victim of a murderer becomes a vampire and haunts his slayer until he is avenged. If a cat or a person leaps over a corpse which is lying in state before burial, the body may become animated.

We need not conclude, however, that the Greeks have borrowed more than the name from the Slavs, for the modern superstition can be shown to go back to the ancient Greek belief in lycanthropy and apparitions. We meet the belief in vampires in parts of Greece where the Slavic immigrants did not penetrate, and they are there called by purely Greek names, which shows that the Greeks had the superstition independently. Thus on Crete and Rhodes a vampire is a *katakhanás, i. e.,* "destroyer," or a *tympaniaîos, i. e.,* "drumhead," the latter name manifestly referring to the swollen condition of the body and its consequently tightly-drawn skin. On Cyprus he is called the *sarkoménos* or "fleshy one," apparently from the fact of his being gorged with food, *i. e.,* blood. On Tenos he is known as the *anakathouménos,* "the snatcher," or, perhaps, "the restless one." But all over the mainland the vampire goes by his Slavic name —a name which appears in varying forms in

[185]

all the Slavic languages of southeastern Europe. In these languages, however, the word does not mean strictly a vampire, but rather a were-wolf or *loup-garou,* although all these peoples believe that were-wolves become vampires. At first the Greeks also used *vrykólakas* in the sense of were-wolf but sometime after the tenth century the word began to denote a vampire, and this is its sole meaning in Greece at present.

The superstition of the were-wolf, lycanthropy, is world-wide and differs essentially from that of the vampire. A were-wolf is merely a man who, for certain reasons, possesses the power to transform himself into animals, into a wild boar in Macedonia, and elsewhere generally into a wolf. Vampires, on the other hand, are *revenants,* dead men returned to life. Since both vampires and were-wolves are fond of blood and murder, and since both at times take on beast forms, they are frequently, but wrongly, confused in the popular mind. We shall trace the two concepts in antiquity and find that both have a good classical origin.

Lycanthropy was a well-known Greek and Latin superstition. Plato, in the *Republic,* recounts an "old tale" that he who tastes of the entrails of a human victim mixed with those of an animal victim at the sacrifice in honor of Zeus Lycæus in Arcadia becomes thereby a wolf. Centuries later, Pausanias, in speaking of the same sacrifice, says that from Lycaon's day onward "a man has always been turned into a wolf at the sacrifice in honor of Lycæan Zeus," but that he may regain his former appearance at the end of nine years, if only he has abstained all that time from eating human flesh. Euanthes, quoted by Pliny, adds another interesting feature to the story to the effect that lots were cast in a certain family, and that he on whom the lot fell became the were-wolf. The man was brought to the edge of a tarn, when he stripped and swam across and fled into desert places, where he lived as a wolf for nine years. At the end of that period he returned to the tarn, swam back, put on his old clothes, and once more became a man. Euanthes also seems to imply that the man had eaten of the human sacrifice; but Pliny, quoting another writer named Scopas, goes on to say that Demænetus, a Parrhasian, tasted the bowel of a boy victim who was slain in honor of Zeus Lycæus and thereby became a wolf. After nine years he became a man again and even won a boxing match at Olympia. St. Augustine tells the same story as that found in Pliny, and quotes Varro as his authority. The latter probably got his information from Euanthes and Scopas. Herodotus tells us that men among the Neuri of eastern Europe became wolves for a few days each year, although, of course, he does not believe the story. Virgil mentions the were-wolf, and Petronius tells quite an extended story of one.

This belief in were-wolves has survived in some degree among the Greeks of to-day. Abbott found that the Macedonian Greeks generally believed that wicked Turks were changed into wild boars at death because of their sins.

As for apparitions, the ancients also believed that the bodies of some men for certain reasons remained undissolved after death and rose from their graves in corporeal form and wandered about. Such apparitions were generally known as *alastores*, "sinners," or, "polluted ones." The causes for such returns were various—the omission of burial rites, violent death, and the commission of deadly sins. Such were in a state midway between life and death, for

[188]

they could walk on earth, but must lie in their graves as dead. Plato, in the *Phædo,* alludes to the belief that the souls of wicked men wander about the grave after death as shadowy ghosts, a belief also mentioned by other Greek and Latin writers. Several ghost stories have come down to us, notably one told by Phlegon, from which, in conjunction with Philostratus' account of the Lamia, Gœthe got the material for *Die Braut von Corinth;* another is told by the younger Pliny,[44] according to which a man long since dead haunted an Athenian house until his bones were actually buried. But such apparitions were not vampires, for these are resuscitated bodies and not ghosts. But the blood craved by the vampire of to-day has its counterpart in the blood craved by the shades of former men in antiquity, to whom human sacrifice was often made. This is the nucleus of the present superstition. Thus the shades evoked by Odysseus in Hades regained temporary vitality by drinking the blood of the sheep slain at the outer trench. In the *Iliad* Achilles slays twelve Trojan youths at the grave of Patroclus. Neoptolemus, in the *Hecuba* of Euripides, immolates the maiden Polyxena in order to appease his father's shade, which is invited to drink her blood. Sophocles has Œdipus say, in reference to a future defeat of Thebes in the neighborhood of his grave, that his cold body will one day drink the warm blood of the slain.

Pausanias tells of the destruction of babies at Corinth by the sons of Medea, because she had been stoned to death. At the command of the oracle annual sacrifices were held in their honor, and a statue of *Terror*, in the likeness of a frightful woman, which Pausanias saw, was set up, and the destruction ceased. The same writer tells a similar story about the devastation of the South Italian town of Temesa by the *Hero*—the spirit of one of Odysseus' companions named Polites, who had been stoned to death there for raping a maiden when he was tipsy. He became a dæmon who preyed on the inhabitants until they in despair were about to seek other homes. The oracle, however, told them to appease the spectre by erecting a temple in his honor and by giving him each year their most beautiful maiden. This spectre was corporeal enough to be finally beaten by the Olympic victor Euthymus, a boxer who had won two victories in 480 and

472 B. C., and who happened to be at Temesa during one of the annual sacrifices. Entering the temple, he saw the chosen damsel, and forthwith fell in love with her. Buckling on his armor he engaged the *Hero* and drove him into the sea, and then married the maiden. Pausanias says that he himself saw a copy of an old painting of the town in which the ghost was represented as a black figure wearing a wolf-skin. In this story he gives a popular account of what probably was the visitation of some form of cholera, common to the regions of South Italy. The townsfolk invented the ingenious story in their effort to attribute the disaster to a malign spirit. Pausanias also tells of a spectre which ravaged the Bœotian city of Orchomenus, until the oracle advised the people to bury the remains of Actæon who had been devoured by his dog, and fashion a bronze statue of the apparition and nail it to a rock. The Periegete says he saw this statue, and it even appears on bronze coins of Orchomenus.

Enough, then, has been said to show that the present Greek vampire has the nucleus of its origin in the ancient superstitions about were-wolves and spectres. But there is one great difference between the old Greek revenants and the modern Romaic vampires. The former were, for the most part, reasonable beings who were not wantonly cruel, chiefly those who had been wronged in life and had returned to work their revenge on enemies. But the latter are beings, like the Ghouls of the *Arabian Nights,* who prey indiscriminately and without justification on all alike. For this characteristic the Greek vampire is certainly indebted to Slavic influence.

The religion of the present day Greeks, then, carries a great burden of amazing survivals of ancient superstitions derived from a dæmonology, much of which goes back even to prehistoric days. Such notions have become so deep-seated and instinctive that neither education nor the power of the Church has been able to eradicate them wholly.

VII. DESTINY, GUARDIAN ANGELS, DEATH, AND THE LIFE HEREAFTER

IN THIS final chapter we shall discuss the modern Greek ideas of destiny, death, and the life hereafter—ideas which we shall find remarkably similar to those held in antiquity.

The belief in the old Fates is still deeply rooted in Greece. Even the ancient name reappears in the modern *Moirais*. They are generally regarded as three dread sisters, wrinkled and infirm, and dressed in black, much as they were described by Hesiod. Only in later antiquity were they artistically pictured as young and beautiful. Sometimes there is only one *Moira*, as there was in the original belief. Again, as on Zante, there are twelve Fates, the chief of whom is the "Queen," who carries a fate-book in her hand containing the fate of every man recorded within. Similarly, Hesiod called Atropus the "oldest and chief" of the Fates. In the Zagori district of Epirus

Schmidt found that one was the spinner of the life-thread, another the apportioner of good fortune, the third of bad fortune. Hesiod has the Fates "give men at their birth both evil and good to have," and the general Greek conception was that Clotho spun, Lachesis apportioned, and Atropus cut the thread of life.

The Fates are still inexorable in their decrees and are even thought of as being independent of God's will. But they are not wantonly cruel, as is shown by the belief that they can be placated. Women, in order to win their favor, often call them "the good ladies," and lay out entertainment for them when they are expected. Thus, on Corfu, Schmidt says that wine, bread, candy, and even money are set out for them, and that sometimes low tables, with three stools about them, are placed in peasants' cottages, upon which honey, almonds, bread, money, and jewels are laid. In Macedonia for the first three nights after a birth, a table, covered with cloth, is set beneath the icon of the Panaghia, and upon it are placed bread, salt, and money; on the third day a second table is set with a honey-cake and a mirror upon it. In Greece, frequently the dog is tied, all furniture is moved out of the way, the house-door is left unlatched, and a light is kept burning. When the Fates enter, silence must be observed and they become angry if they find that proper preparations have not been made against their coming. The commonest offerings are honey and cakes. Thus Dodwell [45] found in the inner room of the rock-cut chamber on the Muses' Hill at Athens, commonly known as the Prison of Socrates, a small feast laid out which consisted of a cup of honey, white almonds, cake, and a vase of burning aromatic herbs. These things had been brought by two Turkish women and placed upon an altar-like rock. He scandalized his attendant by feeding the cake to his donkey, who greedily devoured it without any compunction. It is especially in grottoes and caves that the *Moirais* are supposed to abide, as also on the mountain tops of Olympus and Taÿgetus.

The Fates generally appear at the birth of a child, on one of the three nights thereafter, though they may appear again on the fifth or seventh, when they determine the child's destiny. Just so Apollodorus has them come to Althæa, the mother of Meleager, when the latter was seven days old. In Arachova they write their decrees upon the child's forehead, and if the mother finds any red spots on the child's face, these are left untouched, as they are called the "fating of the Fates." But ordinarily the decrees are set down in the fate-book already mentioned and are irrevocable. A well-known Greek proverb runs: "What the Fate has written on her tablet, no axe can cleave."

The Fates are now the special protectors of women and marriage, as they were in antiquity. Thus Pollux says that the "hair-offering" of brides is for Hera and Artemis and the Fates. Pindar recounts how the Fates led Themis in a golden chariot from Ocean to Olympus to wed Zeus, and Aristophanes says that they sang the marriage-song for Zeus and Hera. Girls before marriage will now place cakes and honey in caves supposed to be haunted by the Fates. Pouqueville [46] says that girls made such offerings in a grotto at the foot of Mount Rigani in Ætolia to find out if they were to marry within the year. If the offering disappeared, the answer was favorable. This recalls a passage in Pausanias in which widows, eager to remarry, are said to have made offerings in a grotto of Aphrodite, which was situated in this same neighborhood. Galt [47] records that Athenian girls on the first night of the full moon placed honey, salt, and bread on a plate beside the Ilissus near the Stadium and in return were promised husbands by the Fates. Women seeking fertility make offerings to the Fates. Pouqueville recounts how such women and those already enceinte used to rub themselves on a rock near the fountain of Callirhöe at Athens and called on the Fates. Wordsworth [48] mentions a grotto at the village of Cephissia near Athens, where peasant women used to resort "to behold their own Moira." A loose fragment falling from the vault indicated that the Fate would be propitious to their prayers. The present offering of honey recalls the statement of Pausanias that the Sicyonians annually made libations of honey and water on the altars of the Eumenides and Fates during their festivals.

The Fates may also be expected at death, although Charus, as we shall see, has usurped most of their functions at that time. On Zante, when a man dies, his "Fates," dressed in black, come and mourn for him; in Arachova, euphemisms of death are used. Thus one hears such expressions as "his thread is cut," or "his spindle is wound full," which show a connection with the ancient Greek idea of the life-thread spun by the Fates.

Side by side with the belief that the Fates fix men's destiny is another notion, common in modern Greece as elsewhere, that a guardian angel is in charge of the human soul, being allotted to it at birth, accompanying it through life, and finally guiding it to God for judgment and thence to heaven or hell. For the soul is often looked upon, as it was in Homer, as issuing from the mouth at death, and it is often pictured as a butterfly or other small winged body, as anciently on the Harpy Tomb of Xanthus. On Cyprus it is believed that the angel stays with the soul for forty days after death before leading it to God. This belief in guardian angels goes back to remote antiquity, when each man was believed to have one, his happiness depending upon the kind allotted to him. The idea passes through many variations. Homer calls such a spirit "Ker," the symbol of death and hate, whose chief purpose was to cause trouble, and the term is woven into the pages of Greek literature of every subsequent period. In the *Iliad* the wraith of Patroclus speaks of his "hateful

Ker," which had been assigned him at his birth, and here the term refers to a concrete fate. But later writers more often call this spirit a dæmon, which can beguile men to virtue or to sin. Pindar speaks of a "natal dæmon," a spirit which watches over a man from his birth. Plato speaks of the genius of each individual to which man belongs in life, and which finally leads him to where the dead are gathered, whence, after judgment, he is guided below. The well-known "dæmon" of Socrates was somewhat different. The philosopher believed that he constantly received warnings of a mantic character through a divine sign. Among the early Church Fathers and the Neo-Platonic thinkers it was assumed that he was attended by a dæmon or genius, and even to-day certain spiritualists have regarded the sign as a guardian spirit. But Xenophon and Plato explicitly show that Socrates did not regard the sign as a divinity or genius. Thus Xenophon says it was a warning to do or not to do and was never disobeyed; Plato says it was a "voice" warning him to refrain from certain courses of action and was peculiar to Socrates. Perhaps the explanation may be found in some hallucination in the sense of hearing, so that

the suggestions of his mind seemed to be pro-
jected beyond him and returned through his ear.
Polydæmonism, or the belief in good and bad
dæmons, was characteristic of the later period
of Greek religion. The same idea of a protecting "genius" was also common in Roman religion. Each man at birth received one, which
was worshipped on birthdays with libations of
wine, with incense, and flowers. Later, during
the Empire, the whole Roman people had its
genius, which is pictured on coins of Trajan
and Hadrian. The idea of a guardian angel
is also found in the Roman Church to-day.

In Greece to-day the angel may be good or
bad; the two are supposed to exist side by side,
the one in conflict with the other for supremacy
in the guidance of a man's life. The bad
angel is sometimes merely the Devil personified. As each in turn may succeed in the
struggle, so is a man's life good or bad. Folk-
songs frequently picture the good angel as giving good advice to a man or helping a woman
in childbirth. But it is easily frightened off
by the bad angel, although it never goes far
away. On Cythnus it is seen only at death,
when a man's broken words during the death
struggle are believed to be addressed to his

angel. If he dies hard, the bad angel is supreme, and vice versa. In some parts a man born on Saturday is believed to be able to see his angel. Similarly, in antiquity it was rare that the protecting genius let itself be seen. The *locus classicus* is found in Plutarch's *Brutus*, where the ghost of the Roman general appeared to him before the fateful battle of Philippi. While the camp was wrapped in silence there came to the warrior a "strange and dreadful apparition, a monstrous and fearful shape," to tell him his immediate fate. When asked who he was the spirit answered, "I am thy evil genius, Brutus, and thou shalt see me at Philippi."

Many present-day funeral customs recall ancient ones both Greek and Roman, though they have been colored by Christian rites. Thus the old custom of carrying the dead uncovered on the bier, which dates back to Solon's law that corpses should be carried to the grave exposed to the chest, is reflected in the present custom of exposing the body in the coffin. Popularly, it is believed that this custom is due to a decree of the Turks, issued long ago to prevent the clandestine transmission of arms. But the fact that it is also observed in the Russian

Orthodox Church disproves any such explanation. Church dignitaries used to be carried to the grave seated upright in their episcopal chairs and robes. The ancient purification after contact with the dead is also seen in the custom, which is still revered on the islands and elsewhere, of throwing an earthen pitcher out of the door to be broken on the steps after the coffin has been carried out. In Arachova pitchers are broken in this way, and on Corfu water is thrown from the windows after the procession has passed. In Maina women still cut off tresses of their hair and throw them into the grave, just as Electra, in Sophocles' drama, invited her sister Chrysothemis to cut one of her locks for the grave of Agamemnon.

Improvised dirges are sung as the corpse is carried out, and again at the grave, by female relatives or by professional wailers, whose business it also is to memorize verses specially composed for the occasion. These recall the *threnodoi* of the women mourners sung about Hector's body.

The present-day funeral feasts are also descended from the classical *perideipnon*. On returning from the grave the mourners are met at the door by a servant who pours lustral water into a basin in which all must lave their hands before re-entering the house. This reminds us of the ancient ablution before the body was carried out. At stated times in Macedonia, on the eighth and fortieth day after burial, or on the anniversary of the death, a memorial feast is celebrated. Then the grave is again decorated with flowers, a mass is sung, and an offering of the *kolyva* or wheaten cakes already discussed, is made at the church, since wheat is the symbol of resurrection. Similarly, in Greece on the third, ninth, and fortieth day, and again six months after death, the *kolyva* are placed on the grave and left, or are divided among the poor. This seems to be a survival of the feast of pots held at the ancient *Anthesteria,* when the Athenians in common boiled vegetables and offered them to Hermes and the chthonian deities.

Perhaps the most widely known superstition of the Greeks is that of Charon, who is now known as Charus or Charondas. Though retaining the old name with little change, the modern Charus is no longer the ferryman of the Styx—that superstition apparently surviving only in one folk-song from Zante—but the personification of Death, who snatches

away souls from mortals and leads them to
the world below. So he has taken over the
function of the Homeric Hades, a name which
no longer refers to a person as it did in Homer,
but rather to the lower world of Charus. Here
Charus dwells with his wife Charondissa, with
his mother and son, the latter being represented
as holding the key of Hades so that none may
escape. Pausanias makes mention of this key
which kept all within the confines of Hades.

Charus is often represented as a tall and
gaunt old man with white hair and claws, cruel
and crafty. Again he is a strong and vigorous
warrior with yellow or black hair, who rides
along the roads on a black horse bearing his
fatal summons. In an island song [49] he appears as a giant whose "look is like the lightning, his complexion like fire, while his
shoulders stand out like two mountains and his
head like a fortress." His raiment is either
black or bright. In another song he is "un-
shod and in glistening raiment, his hair like the
sun and his eyes like lightning." Flashing
eyes are always characteristic of him as they
were of the ancient Charon. In antiquity,
Death was black; thus Euripides calls him the
"sable-vestured king of corpses," and again he

says that "the blackness of death hath shrouded the eyne of the righteous." A famous folk-song, known as "Charus and the Souls," [50] has painted him in most impressive colors. Just as Death in St. John's vision appeared seated upon a pale horse, with Hell following after, and as the Valkyries of Norse legend, so Charus rides along on a black charger driving bands of youthful souls before him, dragging troops of aged souls after him, while on his saddle-bow he carries the souls of little children. And as he passes, the earth quakes beneath the hoofs of his steed, and the mountains are darkened by his shadow. The aged souls beseech him to let them drink at a nearby fountain, but he sternly refuses. This song reminds us of the scene in the *Odyssey,* where Hermes with his wand leads the souls of the suitors down the dank ways, and they follow gibbering. We are also reminded of the story from German poetry of how the father rides through the night-storm with his child at his saddle-bow, and the latter is touched by the Erl-king, although Gœthe derived his inspiration from Danish rather than Greek sources.

It has often been pointed out that there are two concepts in the picture of Charus, the one pagan, the other Christian. According to the one he is merciless and hardhearted, deaf to entreaty and blind to beauty. His usual epithets are "black," "bitter," and "hateful," and he is the equal of God in power, though, unlike him, inexorable. In one distich we read: "Against the wounds that Charus deals, herbs avail not, physicians give no cure, nor saints protection." It is his pleasure to separate mother and child, husband and wife, brother and sister, loved and beloved. "Spare thou mothers who have young children, brothers who have sisters; spare thou also newly wedded pairs." [51] To this appeal of his mother he answers: "Wherever I find three, I carry off two, and where I find two, I carry off one, and when I find one alone, him also I carry off." In the Greek Anthology it was similarly the savage Charon who "cut off a youth from pleasure, not yet knowing wedlock," or insatiably took the lives of youths. In another aspect, however, we see Christian influence. Here Charus is the servant of God, and we even hear of a St. Charus who is charged by God with the duty of escorting souls below and who thus encroaches upon the prerogatives of St. Michael, the successor of Hermes in that

office.   In the songs in which he is represented
as a Christian messenger his character is frequently softened, and he appears unwilling to
snatch away the souls of children, maidens, and
youths.   At times he is even the friend of men,
as in a folk-story recounted by Lawson.   Still
he must do his duty relentlessly, even though
he shifts the responsibility, and says to his
victim that "God has sent me to take thy soul."

Charus often appears as a warrior strong in
archery or in the wrestling art, often, like
Apollo of old, slaying youths with his arrows.
At times he grants delay or accepts a wrestling or leaping match, knowing full well that
he must be victor.   So the death agony in
Greece, as with us, is often euphemistically
called "wrestling with death," and around this
idea have been woven many folk-songs.   In
one of these from Arachova he lies in wait in a
mountain defile for the shepherd Tsopanes, and
suddenly appears to demand his soul.   The
youth suggests a wrestling match on a nearby
threshing-floor, and agrees, if beaten, to forfeit
his life.   For three days and two nights the
bout continues.   On the third day at noon
Charus is injured by a blow, and then in anger
uses unfair means, grasping the shepherd by

the hair and throwing him. The vanquished youth vainly asks for a three-day respite in order to return home once more to feast and drink and take leave of his loved ones. Similarly, Euripides has Heracles wrestle with Death for the life of Alcestis.

Charus as the personification of Death rather than as ferryman of the Styx has led Fauriel to conclude that only the name and not the attributes of the old Charon have survived. In Greek literature Charon is always the ferryman, but the idea is certainly later than Homer and Hesiod. The first literary reference to it seems to have been in the *Minyad,* an epic attributed by Pausanias to Prodicus of Phocæa, and hence not very old. Two lines of this epic, which refer to the descent of Pirithoüs and Theseus into Hell, speak of Charon as ferryman, a scene which Pausanias says was also pictured by Polygnotus in his Delphic painting of the lower world. Æschylus, in the *Seven Against Thebes,* speaks of Charon's "black-sailed galley, sunless, untrodden by Apollo, that leads to the unseen landing-place that is the bourne of all." Euripides and Aristophanes continued the same tradition. But other folklorists have found it more reasonable to derive Charus from popular rather than literary sources of antiquity. Doubtless the popular concept was larger than the one reflected in Greek literature and art, and hence we are justified, perhaps, in following the reasoning of Lawson, Schmidt, and others that Charon originally was Death, a character in which he appears in several late Greek writers. This older non-literary concept, then, did not die out, but has lived on, reappearing in the modern Greek folklore. Schmidt believes that the classical idea of Charon as ferryman came to the Greeks from Egypt, rather than, as has been suggested, from a theater-figure of the Greek drama.[52] On the walls of Etruscan tombs Charon is always represented as the god of death and not as ferryman, either watching at the gate of Hell or leading the dead below, separating relatives and lovers who stretch out their hands to him in fruitless supplication. It is improbable that a mere theater figure should have reached so deeply into the religious consciousness of the Greeks.

The custom of placing a coin in the dead man's mouth has survived, at least until recently, in various parts of Greece. Abbott, Rodd, Miss Hamilton, and others have cited examples of it in Macedonia, Thrace, Albania, and on the Ægean islands. On Zante Schmidt met an old woman who remembered the custom, and at Steinmachus in Thrace he found it still in vogue and that the coin was intended "for Charus." On the Cyclades, and in parts of the mainland Lawson also met people who recalled the custom. Stephani,[53] in 1842, found it in villages beyond Mount Othrys near Lamia. Newton,[54] met it in Macedonia, where Turkish coins were used, but with a Turkish idea in mind, that the money was intended for toll over the "hair-bridge." Near Smyrna the coin so placed was called "passage-money," and consequently it has been referred generally to the ancient Greek custom of placing a coin in the mouth of a corpse to pay the ferryman Charon. Excavators have found coins in the mouths of many corpses of ancient Greeks, the mouth being regarded as the pocket-book of the dead. Bent even records that in his day the obol, mentioned by Lucian and others, was called "boat-money," in a village on Naxos.

But it is doubtful if the modern custom is generally intended for Charus, the present rep-

resentative of Charon. The ancient custom
may have been kept up for quite a different
reason. Sometimes instead of a coin it is a
morsel of bread from the Eucharist which is
laid on the lips of the dead. Again it may be
a piece of pottery on which the Greek letters,
I X NI KA, ('Ιησοῦς Χριστὸς νικᾷ) are
written. In such cases, at least, the custom
can have nothing to do with Charus, but is
intended as a prophylactic against evil spirits,
such as the *Telonia* which we have discussed
in a preceding chapter, or, perhaps, to keep
the soul from reëntering the body as a vampire. The record of Newton about Turkish
coins being used also proves that the custom
in Macedonia cannot have been meant for
Charus. Again it was a key which was laid
upon the dead man's breast; this could not
have been intended, as Schmidt believed, to
open the gates of Paradise, but merely as a
charm. He records that in a cemetery at
Mariais on Zante many Venetian copper coins
and keys have been found among graves which
were at least a century old. On the whole,
then, it seems more logical to conclude that
where the custom has been practiced in modern

times, it is a survival, to be sure, of the ancient one, but with a very different meaning, in part, at least, influenced by Christianity.

The Church for a long time has tried to get rid of this custom, but not always with success. While Schmidt records that in the villages of Cephalonia at the end of the eighteenth century the archbishop of the island was successful in stopping it, Newton tells of the methods used in vain by the archbishop of Mitylene to end the practice in Macedonia by representing that Turkish coins were unfit for Christian graves. The peasants there have gotten round the prohibition by substituting little crosses of wax for the traditional coins.

In conclusion, we shall describe the life hereafter as it appears in the folk-songs and folk-stories of to-day.

Side by side with the Christian idea of Paradise and Hell—the latter being known indifferently as the "place of punishment," "pitch," or even "Tartarus"—the modern Greeks have also retained much of the old Homeric conception, which we have outlined in our opening chapter. Paradise, even as Eden, is a park-like garden with shady trees and cool streams. Tartarus is sometimes a place where brave

pallicars dwell, and again where the wicked
are tied to a fiery wheel which is constantly
turning, a reminiscence of the wheel to which
Hermes tied Ixion for wantonly approaching
Hera, the queen of Heaven. The old word
Hades is often used of the Christian future
world. But to the popular mind Hades is the
realm of Charus, the "lower world," which lies
deep below the earth and is the common home
of all the dead. The ancient notion is still
prevalent that a stream is at its entrance,
which the souls must cross, certainly a reminiscence of Lethe, from which forgetfulness is still
drunk:

*"Where they cross the river and drink the water
    and*
*Become forgetful of their homes and orphaned
    children."*

As caverns and gorges, existing in different
parts of Greece, were anciently regarded as
entrances to Hades, so they are still to-day.
The best known of all is a rock-cavern on the
western side of the promontory of Tænarum—
Cape Matapan—close to the sea. Here the
archangel Michael now appears and releases
the souls which God has forgiven, or leads

others below. It was nearby that Pausanias located the cavern where Heracles descended to bring up Cerberus. On Zante there is a great water-hole known as the "Abyss," which is another entrance. It is regarded by the peasants as bottomless, just as is the Alcyonian pool near Lerna, where Dionysus was anciently believed to have descended into Hell to fetch up Semele. Still another entrance is situated on the southern shore of Zante where the foothills of Mount Scopus rise perpendicularly from the sea. Here, twenty feet above the ground, is a grotto whence a waterfall, called "Thunder-water," issues in winter. Its lonely and difficult position, and the beating of the surf below, lend themselves to the belief, and no peasant will approach it.

In the Romaic folk-tales there are also a few reminiscences of the many-headed dog which once guarded the entrance to Hades. In two tales in the von Hahn collection, one Greek, the other Albanian, this monster is mentioned. In the Albanian story he appears as a "three-headed dog that sleeps not day nor night," but guards the subterranean abode of the "beautiful one." In the Greek story, he appears rather as a three-headed snake, which is ever on guard.   Schmidt also gives a song [55] in which Cerberus appears with all his ancient features and with the added modern touch that Charus is afraid of him.   In this song Charus says: "A savage dog have I, who guards us all, and when he sees me he rages, and would fain devour me.   A three-headed dog is he, and he burns like fire; his claws are sharp and his tail is long; from his eyes he gives forth flame, and from his mouth burning heat; long is his tongue and grim his teeth."   But in most of the songs and tales it is Charus who is on guard, for now he has taken over not only Pluto's duties, but those of Cerberus as well.

To the average Greek of to-day as to the Greek of Homer's time death is the worst of all evils.   The Greeks have no pleasing vision of the future, for Hades is still a gloomy, comfortless, and monotonous place for all who die. There no cock crows, no hen cackles, no water flows, and no grass is found, as the bereaved parents in one song tell their daughter.   The dead long for the sunlight, just as Achilles did. Hades is "icy-cold," or "thick with spiders' webs," epithets which recall Hesiod's phrase, "the mouldering house of chill Hades." Existence below is the very negation of life above, where the hungry cannot eat, nor the thirsty drink, nor the weary sleep. The dead are called "the waterless" and "the thirsty" in the song of a widow. Here there is neither rank nor distinction. In a story from Cephalonia, the wife of Charus is sorry for a fastidious youth who cannot sit except in an arm-chair, nor drink without a glass, nor eat without a napkin, nor sleep without a pillow. But Charus brutally says he will make him accept his lot. Girls are deprived of their ornaments, youths of their weapons, and children of their clothes. Some songs express the wish of the dead that shop-keepers be sent below to supply their needs and thus lighten their woes.

Body and soul, as frequently in Homer, are still identified; for the dead have bodies as they had on earth, even though these are merely the "semblances" (*eidola*) of their earthly existence. Unlike the Homeric dead, they have self-consciousness, feeling, and speech, so that life below is, in one sense, a continuation of life above. In some songs a more comforting picture of this life is given, which recalls the brighter hues found in Pindar's picture of the hereafter. In them marriages are solemnized with music. In a song from Zante we read of the garden of Charus, where he walks amid the cypresses, and where the young girls dance, and the young men sing and play, a scene which recalls the "Blissful Groves" of the *Æneid*, where games, dances, and songs were in order, or the more sensuous picture painted by Tibullus.

Charus is constantly importuned to allow the dead to return and again see the light of day, but he remains ever inexorable. In one song he thus harshly rebukes a young, weeping girl who begs to return and see her little sister for a few years longer: "Here no such gift is made. Do you think you are in a strange land where one can go and come? You are in Hades, my girl, where the dead are. Tell your sister she should not wait for you. When the sea stands still and becomes a garden, and the ravens are metamorphosed into white doves, then first may ye expect to return to earth again." [56] However, against the rule which confines the dead below, we have the Church belief that between Easter and Whitsunday and again on the Saturday before Whitsunday, from midnight till dawn, the dead may revisit the earth. Attempts to get out of Hades are

[217]

recounted in several folk-songs. In one, told
in various versions, the attempt of three brave
youths to escape is described. A lovely
maiden beseeches them to take her along, that
she may revisit her mother and sister or her
child, who have been left behind. The youths
at first refuse as they are afraid lest the rustle
of her dress, the sheen of her hair, the rattle of
her gold and silver ornaments will arrest the
attention of Charus. But at last she is allowed
to accompany them. However, Death meets
them on the way and seizes them all. In one
version, the young mother cries out: "Let
loose my hair, Charus, and take me by the
hand, and if you will give milk to my child, I
shall flee from thee no more." [57]

Another song records how the hero Zachus
rode down to Hell on an iron horse with a
golden saddle in order to visit his friends.
Charus, at first, hides in fear, but later wrestles
with him and is thrown thrice. Finally Charus
is, as usual, victorious, and compels Zachus to
remain below. This fear of Charus recalls
that of Charon who, in the *Æneid*, is frightened at the approach of Heracles, whom he re-
ceives without delay upon his boat.

As Pluto and Persephone jointly rule Erebus

in the Homeric legend, so Charus and Charondissa rule it now. The wife's chief duty now, as queen, is to soothe the frightened new-comers and accustom them to forget their former joys. A tent is their dwelling-place, red outside, but black within, and the tent-poles are the arms of brave youths, and the ropes are the woven-plaits of maidens' hair. At sunset husband and wife sit at table together, and at this time no one on earth must annoy them by bewailing the dead. A story from the island of Thiaki (Ithaca) gives a grim picture of their ghostly meal, since the linen is black, the plates are turned upside down, the heads of children lie upon the table, while their hands are used to take the place of knives and forks. Youths present the cups and maidens delight the king and queen with their songs.

We see, then, that the Homeric conception of Hades and its gloomy surroundings continues among the Greeks of to-day with many modifications, side by side with Christian beliefs, the Church being quite unable to destroy it.

The foregoing sketch has shown us that the religion of ancient Greece has not passed away like a dream, but that in the Christian church and especially in its Eastern branch there continue and survive modes of thought, institutions, and customs which are Greek rather than Jewish in origin.

Much of the primitive grandeur of the teaching of Jesus with its simple and compelling theology and rules of conduct has undergone a marvellous transformation.

In its theology and ethics, Christianity has been profoundly influenced by its contacts with Greek philosophy; in its ritual and hagiology it owes an equal debt to ancient Greek religion, which has also handed over an enormous mass of superstitious beliefs.

We have shown that this influence was inevitable, if Christianity was to make progress on passing from the environment of Palestine to that of the Greek world. In the resultant blend, Christianity has incorporated pagan beliefs and usages, which, though modified, have remained essentially Greek to this day. Much of the primitive Christianity has been changed or been lost altogether. But the process of fusion has been so complete, particularly in the Eastern Orthodox church, that its devotees are both Christian and pagan, almost without consciousness of the fact or of any contradictions.

The spirit of freedom, of harmony, and of happiness that characterized the religion of pagan Greece, outlined in our first chapter, has by a strange irony largely disappeared. The living legacy of ancient Greece to the Christian Church of to-day includes theological and ethical concepts, rites and ceremonies, and, also, alas, a great body of unworthy superstitions. These are so deeply rooted in the folk-consciousness and in the folklore that the church has not been able—even granting its willingness to do so—to throw off these Greek shackles.

Ancient Greece lives on in Eastern Christianity. Nowhere else in life is the vital power of imagination more strikingly exhibited than in the survivals, within the Eastern Church, of pagan theology, ethics, and institutions. This marvellous phenomenon is of first importance in religious history, and this book aims to indicate the vitality and appraise the influence of the old upon the new, of paganism within Greek Christianity.

NOTES AND BIBLIOGRAPHY

NOTES

1. Sophocles, *Fragm.*, 226; Euripides, *Fragm.*, 294, 7.
2. *Iphigenia among the Taurians*, 572.
3. Plato, 246 D. Translation by H. N. Fowler, in *The Loeb Classical Library*, New York, 1919.
4. O. Gruppe, *Griechische Mythologie und Religionsgeschichte*, Munich, 1906; II, pp. 1010–1011.
5. *Odyssey*, XI. 488 ff. (Translation by Butcher and Lang.)
6. On the Eleusinian Mysteries, see P. F. Foucart, *Les Associations religieuses chez les Grecs*, Paris, 1873; *id.*, *Les grands mystères d'Éleusis*, Paris, 1904; H. K. E. de Jong, *Das antike Mysterienwesen*, Leiden, 1909.
7. II. 5. 7.
8. Euripides, *Medea*, 964.
9. *Memorabilia*, I. 3. 3.
10. *Fragm.*, 946.
11. Plato, 279 B; Translation by H. N. Fowler.
12. *Fragm.*, 67; Translation by J. Burnet, *Early Greek Philosophy*, London, 1908 ², p. 152.
13. See *Archives des missions scientifiques et litteraires*, Série 2me, V, pp. 469 ff. (1868).
14. Passow, No. 242.
15. From ἀστραπτο–, and not from ἀστρο–; see Lawson, p. 72.
16. In Arachova they also explain rain by saying that "God is urinating." Similarly, Aristophanes has Strepsiades say that rain was caused by Zeus urinating through a sieve: *Clouds,* 373. The idea of a sieve is still found in parts of Bœotia, where the phrase "God plies his sieve" is used when speaking of hail.

[225]

17. *Monographie de la voie sacrée éleusinienne,* Paris, 1864, pp. 399 ff.

18. Cited by Lawson, pp. 117 ff.

19. See J. Rendel Harris, *The Cult of the Heavenly Twins,* Cambridge, England, 1906, pp. 96–104.

20. *Legenden der heiligen Pelagia,* Bonn, 1879.

21. *Feste der Stadt Athen im Altertum,* Leipzig, 1893, p. 32.

22. "The Modern Carnival . . . in Thrace," in *The Journal of Hellenic Studies,* XXVI. 191–206 (1906).

23. *Golden Bough,* VI, (*The Scapegoat*), London, 1913–15 [3], p. 347.

24. On ancient incubation, see L. Deubner, *De Incubatione,* Leipzig, 1900 [2]; R. Caton, *The Temples and Ritual of Asklepios at Epidaurus and Athens,* London, 1900 [2]; C. R. Simboli, *Disease-Spirits and Divine Cures among the Greeks and Romans* (Diss. inaug.), chapter II, pp. 57 ff., New York, 1921; Sir William Osler, *The Evolution of Modern Medicine,* New Haven, 1922; Mary Hamilton (see Bibliography).

25. VIII. 360 B.

26. *Voyage de la Grèce,* II, p. 170, Paris, 1826–27 [2].

27. On ancient divination see A. Bouché–Leclercq, *Histoire de la divination dans l'antiquité,* I–IV, Paris, 1879-82; W. R. Halliday, *Greek Divination,* London, 1912.

28. See Rodd, pp. 184–5.

29. *De Sacrificiis,* p. 12.

30. Idyll, I. 15 ff.; Translation by J. M. Edmonds, in *The Loeb Classical Library,* New York, 1919.

31. *Fasti,* IV. 761–2.

32. Quoted by Rodd, p. 177.

33. *Reisen auf den griechischen Inseln,* Stuttgart, 1845; III, pp. 181 ff.

34. K. S. Pittakes, in *Archaiologike Ephemeris,* XXX. 648 (1852).

35. *Galatians,* iv, 9.

36. Passow, No. 512, 9–11 (Translation by Lucy Garnett, *Greek Folk Poesy,* p. 81).

37. On the Dracus, see R. M. Dawkins, *Modern*

Greek in Asia Minor. Cambridge, England, 1916, pp. 219 ff.

38. XII. 20.

39. *Erinnerungen und Mittheilungen aus Griechenland,* 1835, No. 12. For the Cyclops story in Modern Greek folk-tales, see Dawkins, *op. cit.,* pp. 217 and 551.

40. *Macedonian Folklore,* p. 75.

41. *Travels in Crete,* London, 1837, chapter 36; cf. Rodd, pp. 195–7.

42. *Travels in North Greece,* London, 1835; III, chapter 38, p. 216

43. *A Voyage into the Levant* (English Translation), London, 1718; I, pp. 103 ff.

44. *Epist.* VII. 27. 5–11. See L. Collison-Morley, *Greek and Roman Ghost Stories,* Oxford, 1912.

45. *A Classical and Topographical Tour through Greece,* London, 1819; I, pp. 396–7.

46. *Voyage de la Grèce,* London, 1826–27 [2]; IV, pp. 46 ff.

47. *Letters from the Levant,* 1813, pp. 109 ff.

48. *Athens and Attica, Journal of a Residence There,* London, 1837 [2], pp. 230 ff.

49. Passow, No. 428.

50. Passow, No. 409; translated by Rodd, p. 286, and others.

51. Passow, No. 408.

52. The steps in the Greek theater which led up from the lower world, and by which ghosts could enter, were called "Charon's Ladder"; Pollux, IV. 132.

53. *Reise durch einige Gegenden des nördlichen Griechenlands,* 1843, p. 38.

54. *Travels and Discoveries in the Levant,* London, 1865; I, p. 289.

55. *Maerchen,* Song No. 39; translation by Lawson, p. 100.

56. Schmidt, *Volksleben,* p. 242.

57. Passow, No. 424.

BIBLIOGRAPHY

A. On Ancient Greek Religion:

ADAM, JAMES, *The Religious Teachers of Greece.*
Edinburg, 1908.

CAMPBELL, L., *Religion in Greek Literature.* London,
1898.

DICKINSON, G. LOWES, *The Greek View of Life* (Chapter I). London, 1907 [6].

FAIRBANKS, ARTHUR, *Handbook of Greek Religion.*
New York, 1910.

FARNELL, L. R., *Cults of the Greek States.* I–V. Oxford, 1896–1921.

FARNELL, L. R., *Higher Aspects of Greek Religion.* New
York, 1912.

HARRISON, J. E., *The Religion of Ancient Greece*
(Primer). London, 1905.

HARRISON, J. E., *Prolegomena to the Study of Greek
Religion.* Cambridge, England, 1908 [2].

HASTINGS, J., *Encyclopedia of Religion and Ethics.*
New York, 1908–1922: *Ægean Religion* (D. G. Hogarth), I, 141 ff.; *Greek Religion* (L. R. Farnell), VI, 392
ff.

HYDE, W. W., *The Religion of Greece* (in J. A. Montgomery, *Religions of the Past and Present,* pp. 244–315,
Philadelphia, 1918).

INGE, W. R., *Religion* (in R. W. Livingstone, *The Legacy of Greece.* Oxford, 1922).

MAURY, L. F. A., *Histoire des religions de la Grèce antique.* I–III. Paris, 1857–1859. (the most readable history).

MEYER, E., *Geschichte des Altertums,* II–IV. Stuttgart, 1893–1902. (the best historical account in relation to
politics, society, and economics).

MOORE, C. H., *The Religious Thought of the Greeks*

from Homer to the Triumph of Christianity. Cambridge, Massachusetts, 1916.

MOORE, G. F., *History of Religions.* New York, 1920 [2]; I, pp. 406–539.

MORE, PAUL ELMER, *The Religion of Plato.* Princeton, 1921.

MURRAY, SIR GILBERT, *Four Stages of Greek Religion.* New York, 1912.

ROHDE, E., *Psyche.* Tuebingen, 1903 [3].

STENGEL, P., *Die griechischen Kultusaltertuemer.* Munich, 1920 [3].

B. On Survivals:

ABBOTT, G. F., *Macedonian Folklore.* Cambridge, England, 1903; *Songs of Modern Greece* (with Introduction, Translation, and Notes). Cambridge, 1900.

ALLATIUS, LEO (Allacci Leone), *De Græcorum hodie quorundam opinationibus.* Cologne, 1645.

BENT, J. THEODORE, *The Cyclades; or Life among the Insular Greeks.* London, 1885.

DELEHAYE, PÈRE HIPPOLYTE, *Legends of the Saints.* London, 1907.

FAURIEL, CLAUDE CHARLES, *Chansons populaires de la Grèce moderne* (avec une traduction française). Paris, 1824–5.

FRAZER, SIR J. G., *Pausanias's Description of Greece.* I-VI. Reprinted. London, 1914.

GARNETT, LUCY M. J., *Greek Folk Poesy* (with annotated translations). I–II. London, 1896; *Greece of the Hellenes* (Chapter XIV). London and New York, 1914.

HAHN, J. G. VON, *Griechische und Albanesische Maerchen,* I–II. Leipzig, 1864.

HAMILTON, MARY, *Greek Saints and their Festivals.* London, 1910; *Incubation: or the Cure of Disease in Pagan Temples and Christian Churches.* London, 1906.

HATCH, E., *The Influence of Greek Ideas and Usages upon the Christian Church,* edited A. M. Fairbairn. London, 1891 [3].

LAWSON, J. C., *Modern Greek Folklore and Ancient Greek Religion.* Cambridge, England, 1910.

BIBLIOGRAPHY

LEGRAND, ÈMILE, *Recueil, de Chansons Populaires Grecques*. Paris, 1874.

PASSOW, A., *Popularia Carmina Graeciae recentioris*. Leipzig, 1860.

POLITES, N., Μελέτη ἐπὶ τοῦ βίου τῶν νεωτέρων Ἑλλήνων. Athens, 1871, (Summarized by Èmile Legrand, in *La mythologie, neo-Hellénique*, Paris, 1872.); *id.*, Παραδόσεις, I-II Athens.

RODD, SIR JAMES RENNELL, *The Customs and Lore of Modern Greece*. London, 1892.

SCHMIDT, B., *Griechische Maerchen, Sagen, und Volkslieder*. Leipzig, 1877; *Das Volksleben der Neugriechen und das Hellenische Altertum*. I. Leipzig, 1871.

Other works are cited in the *Notes*.

In writing the present book I wish to express my indebtedness to the works of Abbott, Hamilton, Hatch, Passow, Rodd, Schmidt, and especially Lawson, which I have used freely.

Our Debt to Greece and Rome

AUTHORS AND TITLES

HOMER. *John A. Scott.*

SAPPHO. *David M. Robinson.*

EURIPIDES. *F. L. Lucas.*

ARISTOPHANES. *Louis E. Lord.*

DEMOSTHENES. *Charles D. Adams.*

THE POETICS OF ARISTOTLE. *Lane Cooper.*

GREEK RHETORIC AND LITERARY CRITICISM. *W. Rhys Roberts.*

LUCIAN. *Francis G. Allinson.*

CICERO AND HIS INFLUENCE. *John C. Rolfe.*

CATULLUS. *Karl P. Harrington.*

LUCRETIUS AND HIS INFLUENCE. *George Depue Hadzsits.*

OVID. *Edward Kennard Rand.*

HORACE. *Grant Showerman.*

VIRGIL. *John William Mackail.*

SENECA THE PHILOSOPHER. *Richard Mott Gummere.*

APULEIUS. *Elizabeth Hazelton Haight.*

MARTIAL. *Paul Nixon.*

PLATONISM. *Alfred Edward Taylor.*

ARISTOTELIANISM. *John L. Stocks.*

STOICISM. *Robert Mark Wenley.*

LANGUAGE AND PHILOLOGY. *Roland G. Kent.*

AUTHORS AND TITLES

AESCHYLUS AND SOPHOCLES. *J. T. Sheppard.*

GREEK RELIGION. *Walter Woodburn Hyde.*

SURVIVALS OF ROMAN RELIGION. *Gordon J. Laing.*

MYTHOLOGY. *Jane Ellen Harrison.*

ANCIENT BELIEFS IN THE IMMORTALITY OF THE SOUL. *Clifford H. Moore.*

STAGE ANTIQUITIES. *James Turney Allen.*

PLAUTUS AND TERENCE. *Gilbert Norwood.*

ROMAN POLITICS. *Frank Frost Abbott.*

PSYCHOLOGY, ANCIENT AND MODERN. *G. S. Brett.*

ANCIENT AND MODERN ROME. *Rodolfo Lanciani.*

WARFARE BY LAND AND SEA. *Eugene S. McCartney.*

THE GREEK FATHERS. *James Marshall Campbell.*

GREEK BIOLOGY AND MEDICINE. *Henry Osborn Taylor.*

MATHEMATICS. *David Eugene Smith.*

LOVE OF NATURE AMONG THE GREEKS AND ROMANS. *H. R. Fairclough.*

ANCIENT WRITING AND ITS INFLUENCE. *B. L. Ullman.*

GREEK ART. *Arthur Fairbanks.*

ARCHITECTURE. *Alfred M. Brooks.*

ENGINEERING. *Alexander P. Gest.*

MODERN TRAITS IN OLD GREEK LIFE. *Charles Burton Gulick.*

ROMAN PRIVATE LIFE. *Walton Brooks McDaniel.*

GREEK AND ROMAN FOLKLORE. *William Reginald Halliday.*

ANCIENT EDUCATION. *J. F. Dobson.*